Cambridge Elements

Elements in Religion and Monotheism
edited by
Paul K. Moser
Loyola University Chicago
Chad Meister
*Affiliate Scholar, Ansari Institute for Global Engagement with Religion,
University of Notre Dame*

AFRICAN PHILOSOPHY OF RELIGION AND WESTERN MONOTHEISM

Kirk Lougheed
LCC International University/University of Pretoria

Motsamai Molefe
University of South Africa

Thaddeus Metz
University of Pretoria

CAMBRIDGE
UNIVERSITY PRESS

Shaftesbury Road, Cambridge CB2 8EA, United Kingdom

One Liberty Plaza, 20th Floor, New York, NY 10006, USA

477 Williamstown Road, Port Melbourne, VIC 3207, Australia

314–321, 3rd Floor, Plot 3, Splendor Forum, Jasola District Centre, New Delhi – 110025, India

103 Penang Road, #05–06/07, Visioncrest Commercial, Singapore 238467

Cambridge University Press is part of Cambridge University Press & Assessment, a department of the University of Cambridge.

We share the University's mission to contribute to society through the pursuit of education, learning and research at the highest international levels of excellence.

www.cambridge.org
Information on this title: www.cambridge.org/9781009524933

DOI: 10.1017/9781009524919

First published 2024

A catalogue record for this publication is available from the British Library.

ISBN 978-1-009-52493-3 Hardback
ISBN 978-1-009-52489-6 Paperback
ISSN 2631-3014 (online)
ISSN 2631-3006 (print)

African Philosophy of Religion and Western Monotheism

Elements in Religion and Monotheism

DOI: 10.1017/9781009524919
First published online: February 2024

Kirk Lougheed
LCC International University/University of Pretoria

Motsamai Molefe
University of South Africa

Thaddeus Metz
University of Pretoria

Author for correspondence: Kirk Lougheed, philosophy@kirklougheed.com

Abstract: The Abrahamic faiths of Christianity, Judaism, and Islam are typically recognized as the world's major monotheistic religions. However, African Traditional Religion is, despite often including lesser spirits and gods, a monotheistic religion with numerous adherents in sub-Saharan Africa; it includes the idea of a single most powerful God responsible for the creation and sustenance of everything else. This Element focuses on drawing attention to this major world religion that has been much neglected by scholars around the globe, particularly those working in the West or Northern Hemisphere. It accomplishes this primarily by bringing it into conversation with topics in the Anglo-American philosophy of religion.

Keywords: African philosophy of religion, global philosophy of religion, comparative philosophy of religion, philosophy of religion, global religious ethics

ISBNs: 9781009524933 (HB), 9781009524896 (PB), 9781009524919 (OC)
ISSNs: 2631-3014 (online), 2631-3006 (print)

Contents

1 Towards a Global Philosophy of Religion

The Abrahamic faiths of Christianity, Judaism, and Islam are typically recognized as the world's major monotheistic religions. However, African Traditional Religion is, despite often including lesser spirits and gods, a monotheistic religion with numerous adherents in sub-Saharan Africa; it includes the idea of a single most powerful God responsible for the creation and sustenance of everything else. This Element focuses on drawing attention to this major world religion that has been much neglected by scholars around the globe, particularly those working in the West or Northern Hemisphere. It accomplishes this primarily by bringing it into conversation with topics in the Anglo-American philosophy of religion.

This Element begins by highlighting the key claims of African Traditional Religion in order both to introduce unfamiliar readers to it and to distinguish it from other monotheistic religions (Section 2. After that, a number of arguments for and against the existence of God will be examined with an eye to exploring how they fare on African Traditional Religion (Sections 3 and 4). The Element then highlights unique aspects of morality that can be derived from African Traditional Religion (Section 5), and implications for the afterlife (Section 6), before concluding with some general remarks about globalizing the philosophy of religion.

1.1 Motivation

Professional philosophers of religion working in the 'Western' or 'Anglo-American' tradition (more on these labels later) in the post-WWII era have largely focused on the Abrahamic faiths, with the Judeo-Christian conception of God often taking centre stage (if only implicitly). There is nothing wrong with this in and of itself. However, there are likely important epistemic insights to be gained if more religious traditions were included in Anglo-American theorizing (Lougheed 2022). After all, why think that only one tradition has fastened onto religious truths or justified beliefs? It is more plausible to think that insight into the human condition is distributed across many long-standing intellectual traditions, even if to varying degrees. Alternative forms of theism such as pantheism, panentheism, and polytheism emerge as obvious candidates for consideration. Eastern traditions such as Hinduism, Buddhism, and Jainism, among others, also naturally suggest themselves for consideration. Though the field of Anglo-American philosophy of religion is slowly becoming more global,[1] African Traditional Religion remains largely ignored.[2]

Our motivation in writing this Element is to help remedy this situation by providing an accessible critical introduction to African Traditional Religion that points to a number of philosophical topics ripe for fruitful cross-cultural dialogue with the Anglo-American tradition. We wish to show that there are epistemic insights to be gained if various debates in the Anglo-American philosophy of religion were to begin to include African Traditional Religion in their discussion. Just how different is African Traditional Religion from Christianity or other forms of Western monotheism? When it is considered in debates about the existence of God or religious ethics, what, if anything, changes? What we hope to show by addressing these and related questions is that there is much to be gained from continuing to globalize the field of philosophy of religion by including insights from African Traditional Religion.

1.2 Geographic Labels: What Makes an Idea African or Western?

The labels 'African' and 'Western' are often vexed, and it is beyond our purposes to enter into substantive debate about how best they should be used, if at all. Briefly, however, we believe that whether an idea counts as African or Western is a matter of degree (Metz 2022, 7–12). To say that an idea is African is just to say that has been particularly salient on the continent for an extended period of time and to large groups of people in various parts of it. We further submit that the ideas we ascribe to African Traditional Religion in Section 2 have indeed been salient for an extended period of time and for many people on the continent. This does not commit us to any claims of universal agreement in religious belief or practice across the continent.

Scepticism about the use of geographical labels may remain. Are there recent, in-depth, sociological studies about the beliefs of most Africans south of the Sahara that are not infected with colonial biases? What is the term 'Western' supposed to be west of? If we label something 'African', what does that mean for individuals on the continent who do not share those features?

For readers who share these worries, they can read our claims as applying merely to the work of academic exponents of African Traditional Religion in

---

[1] Recent calls to globalize the discipline can be found in Draper and Schellenberg (2018) and Lougheed (2022), among other places. A multimillion-dollar research grant awarded to Yujin Nagasawa (University of Birmingham) to work on the global philosophy of religion of religion marks a watershed moment. See The Global Philosophy of Religion Project, University of Birmingham (global-philosophy.org).

[2] It is a welcome development that some recent exceptions are beginning to emerge.

post-independent Africa, and about the body of literature in philosophy of religion primarily conducted in English since WWII. While we believe that many Africans do hold the beliefs we describe in Section 2, as philosophical proponents of African Traditional Religion did not conjure it up out of nowhere, and that what 'Western' and 'Anglo-American' refer to in this context are sufficiently clear, the reader may read our claims as more narrowly focused on what academic exponents, particularly professional philosophers, say about these topics post-WWII and post-independence.

1.3 Conclusion

This Element does not assume prior knowledge of either African philosophy of religion or the Anglo-American philosophy of religion. Those with knowledge of the former may wish to skip Section 2. Furthermore, though the Element is intended to make up a coherent whole, all sections are relatively self-contained such that they can be read on their own, especially by those with relevant background knowledge. We hope that this Element will make a significant contribution towards expanding the philosophy of religion into a truly global field. Whether new to the philosophy of religion or an experienced practitioner, there will be much food for thought in the following pages.

1.4 Section Summaries

Section Two: What Is African Traditional Religion?

This section introduces the reader to the main features of African Traditional Religion in order to set the stage for the rest of the Element. While there are clear similarities between it and the Abrahamic faiths, this section focuses on highlighting the unique features of African Traditional Religion as compared to them. These include the ideas that God is distant from humans, created the universe *ex materia*, and literally all concrete objects are imbued with vital force. This force explains the African hierarchy of being in addition to the fundamental unity and interconnectedness of everything in the universe. This interconnectedness is extended to the living dead (those who have recently died but whose selves remain on Earth) and long departed ancestors, thereby explaining the closeness of those imperceptible agents (or 'spirits') to human beings.

Section Three: Arguments for the Existence of God

This section examines three arguments for the existence of God, namely, the cosmological argument and the teleological argument. It argues that the former cannot be used to demonstrate the existence of God as conceived of by African

Traditional Religion, since on this view God does not create the world from nothing. Versions of the teleological argument, however, can be defended on African Traditional Religion. Indeed, shaping pre-existing matter may be more plausible than designing something out of material one created out of nothing or at least a comparably great feat. African traditional religion tends to emphasize the interconnectedness of everything that exists (both animate and apparently inanimate objects), and this idea may serve to strengthen teleological considerations in support of God's existence.

Section Four: Arguments against the Existence of God

This section examines two arguments against the existence of God, namely, the problem of divine hiddenness, the problem of no best world, and the evidential problem of evil. This section suggests that there are unique and previously unexplored responses to the problem of divine hiddenness when examined from African Traditional Religion. For example, in African Traditional Religion, God is typically thought to be quite distant from humans because God is so wholly different. Divine hiddenness is less of a surprise for African Traditional Religion than more Western conceptions of monotheism. With respect to the problem of evil, this section explores whether certain responses to it offered in the Anglo-American literature are compatible with African Traditional Religion. For example, sceptical theism is the response that humans are not in a good epistemic position to identify whether a particular instance of evil is gratuitous because they are not in a good position to identify possible reasons God has for permitting that evil. In African Traditional Religion given that God is typically understood to be even more distant from humans and inscrutable, sceptical theism might be even more plausible. On the other hand, soul-making theodicies may be untenable because according to African Traditional Religion, humans do not have souls (in the Western sense), nor is there an eternally good afterlife.

Section Five: African Religious Ethics

Supposing the defining onto-moral feature of God is vitality rather than rationality, what might this consideration mean for religious ethics? Vitality is an imperceptible divine energy that originates and maximally inheres in God, who has since distributed it to all that concretely exist. By 'religious ethics' this section will limit its scope to the concept of moral status, including human dignity, and its applications to bioethical questions involving the beginning of life (abortion) and the end of life (euthanasia). It will contrast vitality ethics and its implications for bioethics with the dominant Christian view of human dignity and its implications for the bioethical questions of abortion and euthanasia.

Section Six: The Afterlife

The conception of the afterlife one generally finds in the Abrahamic faiths stands in stark contrast to descriptions of the afterlife in ATR. On the former, many hold that there is an indestructible soul such that the self necessarily lives forever, while on the latter it is natural to think that if one is made up of vital energy, and furthermore dependent on others for its sustenance, eventually it will break down. In this section, we explain the differences in these conceptions of the afterlife before explaining their implications for the debate about the meaning of life. We suggest that the type of afterlife posited by ATR, which in effect is a kind of life-extension in an imperceptible realm on Earth, has not been sufficiently explored in connection to meaning and other areas of value theory.

2 What Is African Traditional Religion?

2.1 Introduction

This section introduces the reader to some of the main characteristics of African Traditional Religion (from here on also 'ATR'). This includes an explanation of the most important divine attributes, the nature of creation, the interconnectedness and hierarchy implied by the existence of life force or vital energy, the key ontological categories, and the nature of death and immortality, among others. This section is intended primarily as informational and stage-setting for the rest of the Element, and as such we focus on highlighting features that differ from the Abrahamic faiths. This will set the stage for our cross-cultural analysis and debate in the remaining sections.

Before proceeding it is important to recognize that ATR is an umbrella term representing a kind of synthesis of religious views located on the African continent. It is normally used to represent areas of widespread, though not unanimous, agreement, and hence is not to deny the diversity of religious belief across the continent. Typically religious activity and belief are understood as a part of everyday life, with no distinction made between the religious and the secular by indigenous peoples. This can make formulating a set of explicit beliefs associated with ATR somewhat forced; however, it is necessary for the purposes of our project and as a way to advance scholarship on African philosophy of religion in general.

2.2 Divine Attributes and Divine Creation

Similar to the Abrahamic faiths, ATR typically says that there is one God who is the most powerful, good, and knowing person. God is responsible for creating and sustaining all else that exists. One important view of God understands him to consist essentially of the most powerful vital force, an invisible energy, with all else in the world being an offshoot of God. God is also often thought to be eternal, distant, imperceptible, and in some important sense unknowable (Mbiti 1975, 53–5). However, unlike in the Abrahamic faiths, some scholars hold that God is instead said to create *ex materia*, not *ex nihilo*. This means that God creates the universe out of eternal pre-existing matter (more on this in Section 3).[3]

2.3 Interconnectedness

One feature that clearly delineates ATR from the Abrahamic faiths is the emphasis that many scholars place on the interconnectedness between a vital God and the rest of the created universe. Interconnectedness exists because all things that exist, both animate and inanimate objects, are imbued with vital force or vital energy (Anyanwu 1984, 90; see also Imafidon 2014a, 144; Unah 2014, 109). Some forces inhere in what is perceptible, while other forces are in the imperceptible dimension of God and ancestors. The omnipresent existence of vital energy explains why ATR is said to possess a high degree of ontological unity (e.g., Behrens 2014, 55; Chemhuru 2014, 8), contrasting with the phys-ical/spiritual dualism of Cartesianism and more generally the Abrahamic faiths (see 1.5). Forces are constantly pushing and pulling in interaction with each other, both within and between realms. Sometimes a spider web analogy is invoked, such that a change in the direction or strength of force in one area affects both perceptible and imperceptible forces elsewhere.

2.4 Hierarchy

Vital energy as constitutive of everything implies what is known as the 'African hierarchy of being' or the 'African chain of being'. As the creator of the universe, all vital energy comes from God (Anyanwu 1984, 92–5; see also Bujo 2005; Kasenene 1994; Magesa 1997). God has the most vital force and has chosen to place humans at the centre of the visible universe (Dzobo 1992, 224; Uzukwu 1982, 194–5). Humans have the most force of what is perceptible on Earth, but not as much as lesser gods or departed ancestors (Gbadegesin 1991, 112–3) who exist imperceptibly. Though forces constantly interact with each other, only stronger forces can impact weaker ones. Finally, the living dead and departed ancestors are thought to remain nearby in order to act as a conduit to God so that they can transfer vital energy to those who are still alive (e.g., Hamminga 2005, 58). Another facet of the great chain of being is that moral status or at least final goodness tracks the degree and complexity of vital force,

---

[3] The view that God creates *ex materia* is often, though not exclusively, associated with the limited-God view (see 2.8).

making humans the most important perceptible beings on Earth, with plants and animals being less important but having their own inherent value.[4]

2.5 The Invisible and the Visible

Though Westerners, including those working in the Anglo-American philosophy of religion, will often draw firm lines between the 'spiritual' and 'physical' or the 'immaterial' and 'material' or 'other worldly' and 'this world', it is worth emphasizing that such distinctions are not to be found in ATR. Instead, this tradition draws a distinction between the 'visible' and 'invisible' where both are thought to exist in very much the same all-inclusive realm (e.g., Gbadegesin 1991, 85). For example, the living dead, persons whose human bodies have recently died, are understood to continue to exist in the world, alongside those who are still living as human beings (e.g., Bujo 2001, 85; Ehiakhamen 2014, 98). They are not located in some remote or distinct plane of existence, but instead at a gravesite, in the countryside, or perhaps reincarnated within the body of a newborn infant. Finally, it should be reiterated that vital energy and the interconnectedness of all that exists stretches across the visible plane to the invisible plane. This binds not only living humans together, but also living humans together with the living dead, departed ancestors, 'spirits', and ultimately, with God (Mulago 1991, 120; Sindima 1989, 538).

2.6 Death, Immortality, the Living Dead, and Ancestors

With respect to death and immortality, ATR sometimes claims that God originally gave humans immortality but that it was somehow lost. One common myth says that the animal messenger sent by God to deliver immortality never arrived and so a second animal messenger arrived instead with a message of mortality (Mbiti 1975, 110). Other myths are close to the one found in the book of Genesis of the Torah or Bible, where mortality is said to be a punishment from God.

In ATR, death is sometimes said to be caused by sorcery, witchcraft, evil spirits, or curses (Mbiti 1975, 111–2). When a person dies, they become part of the 'living dead', remaining very much a part of their community, though in the invisible dimension. The living dead retain personal identity for as long as they are remembered and otherwise honoured and supported by relatives (Mbiti 1975, 119). If they are engaged with long enough, and if they had done much to support the vital force of the clan, they reach the venerated status of

---

[4] The ideas of interconnectedness and hierarchy offer a metaphysical explanation for why the idea and ideal of community is crucial among African social, moral, and political theory.

a departed ancestor.[5] There is usually no conception of immortality as in Christianity and Islam, with personal identity evaporating once the deceased person is forgotten by their relatives, typically after four or five generations.[6]

The living dead and especially departed ancestors are important because they mediate between God and humans. This explains why Westerners have sometimes mistakenly attributed ancestor worship to Africans. Praying and otherwise attending to ancestors is a way to access an otherwise distant and remote God; they are not being worshipped in the Western sense (Mbiti 1975, 125) (see also Menkiti 1984; Murove 2007). In addition, while it is true that Africans routinely ask ancestors for help and consider them (having greater vital force) to be higher than we are, those are signs of respect as opposed to deification.

2.7 Divine Gender and Pronouns

It is worth briefly explaining that we use male pronouns for God throughout this Element for the simple reason that these are the pronouns almost universally used for God throughout the contemporary philosophical and theological literature on ATR. Though it is open for debate whether expositors of ATR would attribute a literal gender or sex to God, this is not a topic that has been explored in any detail, with the little African feminist theology that has been conducted so far being almost entirely focused on Christianity (but see Attoe 2022: 15–40 for the view that 'it' is apt for God). Debates about divine pronouns have recently emerged in the Anglo-American philosophy of religion, but instead of pursuing the topic further we just observe that this is an area to consider for future research (e.g., Rea 2016).

2.8 The African Limited-God

We have thus far implied that there is common ground between ATR and the Abrahamic faiths in all holding to a monotheistic conception of God that says that he is the most knowledgeable, powerful, and moral. Where these involve the omniproperties, we will call this conception of God the 'maximal God' or 'omni-God' throughout the rest of this Element. However, before concluding this section, it is important to observe some exponents of ATR deny that an omni-description of God is accurate. Consider what Kwasi Wiredu (1931–2022), a leading figure in contemporary African philosophy, writes about discussions of religion in Africa when he claims that:

---

[5] While we will refer to the difference between the living dead and ancestors throughout this Element, we note that there is disagreement amongst the authors about whether there really is a substantive difference between these notions.

[6] We are assuming that personal identity is necessary for immortality. See Menkiti (1984, 174–5), Ramose (1999, 65–6).

[M]any African writers on African religions, proud of their African identity [...] suggest that their peoples recognize the same God as the Christians, since God is one. The origin of this tendency seems to me to be the following: almost all these writers are themselves Christians, in most cases divines. Being scandalized by the opinion of some of the early European visitors to Africa that the African was too primitive to attain the belief in God unaided, they have sought to demonstrate that Africans discovered God on their own before a European or any foreigner, for that matter, set foot in Africa. However, since they themselves have been brought up to think that the Christian God is the one true God, it has been natural for them to believe that the God of their ancestors is, in fact, the same as the God of Christianity. Furthermore, they have been able to satisfy themselves that, in accepting Christianity, they have not fundamentally forsaken the religion of their ancestors. (Wiredu 1998, 37)

Thus, one reason to be sceptical of an omni-description of ATR is based on the claim that early exponents of ATR tended to be Christians and/or have colonial motivations (Agada 2022a, 1; see also Idowu 1973; Mbiti 1975; Metuh 1981). There thus emerged calls to decolonize the African philosophy of religion, and in particular to remove from it the undue influence of Christian thinking (e.g., Balogun 2009; Bewaji 1998; p'Bitek 1971; Sogolo 1993; Wiredu 1998).

Many who advocate for the decolonial project deny that the African God is omniscient, omnipotent, and omnibenevolent. Instead, God is said to be the most powerful and the most knowledgeable being in existence, but not one with unlimited or maximal knowledge and power. We will call this conception of God the 'limited-God' throughout the rest of this Element. One particularly recent and interesting example of the limited-God thesis claims that God's ability to create the world out of pre-existing matter or energy shows that he is the most powerful and knowledgeable *vital*-God.

In this Element we will work with the interpretation of ATR that shares the maximal God in common with the Abrahamic faiths. Ada Agada persuasively argues that *both* understandings of God can be supported within the tradition of ATR:

If it is asserted that 'There exists a Supreme Being that is omnipotent, omniscient, and omnibenevolent', evidence can be extracted from African oral sources that both prove and disprove the assertion. If it is also asserted that 'There is no transcendent God but only a limited deity that cannot stop the evil in the world', both corroborating and discrediting evidence can be extracted from African oral sources. (Agada 2022a, 2–3)

The omni-God is therefore just one prominent strand of ATR, and we believe there are multiple approaches one could take to this sort of project. However, it is a matter of simplicity that in a short Element, we cannot consider both conceptions of the omni-God and limited-God extensively. It would be a disservice to scholarship on the limited-God to attempt to discuss it here. We believe that it will be evident that, even with agreement on properties such as omniscience, omnibenevolence, and omnipotence, there is still much divergence across these traditions that make important comparative work possible.[7] We will strive to highlight places for the reader where the limited-God would make a difference to the argument or topic in question, mostly to observe places for future work.

2.9 Conclusion

Luis Cordeiro-Rodrigues and Ada Agada observe that in the African philosophy of religion, 'the existence of God tends to be assumed (Mbiti 1990) [...] the African theistic conception of God is qualified with African concepts; but this African conception of God is not significantly different from how God is understood in Western theistic circles' (Cordeiro-Rodrigues and Agada 2022, 4). This explains, at least in part, the relative dearth of scholarship on arguments for and against the existence of God in ATR (with the very recent discussion of the problem of evil a notable exception). This observation motivates us to begin to fill in some of these gaps by examining some of the classical arguments for and against God's existence in the context of ATR in Sections 3 and 4. Finally, the reader will notice that our description of ATR in general, and of the importance of vital energy in particular, has clear ethical implications. However, we intentionally do not address moral implications in this section, as we devote all of Section 5 to them. Discussions of contemporary African ethics are decidedly secular or at least rarely invoke God's will, and so there is much fertile ground for an examination of African religious ethics.

To reiterate, the purpose of this section has been to introduce the reader to the basic features of ATR. While there are clear similarities between them, including the omniproperties of some versions of ATR, this section has otherwise focused on highlighting the unique features of ATR as compared to the Abrahamic Faiths. These include the idea that God is distant from humans, created the universe *ex materia*, and that literally everything is imbued with vital energy. This energy explains the African hierarchy of being, in addition to the fundamental unity and interconnectedness of everything in the universe. This interconnectedness is extended to the living dead and departed ancestors, thereby explaining the closeness of those persons in the invisible realm to us. With this background in view, we now turn to analysing what some of these

---

[7] We believe that this Element is proof that it is a fruitful approach even if it turns out not to be the best one.

unique features entail for certain debates in contemporary Anglo-American philosophy of religion.

3 Arguments for the Existence of God

3.1 Introduction

This section examines two arguments for the existence of God, specifically the cosmological argument and the teleological argument. It argues that the former cannot be used to demonstrate the existence of God as conceived of on ATR since on this view God does not create the world from nothing. The standard cosmological argument is lost on ATR. However, the teleological argument can be defended on ATR. Indeed, shaping pre-existing matter may be a more realistic type of design than designing something out of nothing and could count as a comparable great-maker. Finally, the emphasis found in ATR on the interconnectedness of everything that exists may pave the way towards a new teleological argument in support of God's existence.

3.2 The Cosmological Argument

As with virtually all arguments in natural (a)theology, the cosmological or 'first-cause' argument really represents a cluster of related arguments. Versions of the cosmological argument can be found all the way back to the ancient Greeks, including in Plato (*The Laws, X*) and Aristotle (*Physics, VIII*). Cosmological arguments have also been defended by important figures in the history of philosophy such as Thomas Aquinas (*Summa Theologiae*, I, Q. 2, art. 3), Samuel Clarke (1705 (1998) §8–12), and Gottfried Leibniz (1714 (1991) §32–36). There are also contemporary proponents of the argument (e.g., Craig 1979; Swinburne 1979), with its success remaining a matter of considerable debate (e.g., Oppy 2002, 2006; Morriston 2003). In this section, we examine how two different versions of the cosmological argument – one that relies on the Principle of Sufficient Reason and one that does not – fare on ATR.

3.2.1 The Principle of Sufficient Reason and the Cosmological Argument

While acknowledging that there are numerous different versions of the cosmological argument, William Rowe explains that if all of them rely on some underlying principle that could be shown to be false, then *all* cosmological arguments would fail (1968, 279). Rowe contends that one such principle might be the Principle of Sufficient Reason (from here on 'the PSR'). While cosmological arguments and their connection to the PSR have been hotly debated since the time of Rowe's comments, we will work with his version of the argument for the sake of simplicity (e.g., Almeida 2018; Pruss 2006; Pruss and Gale 2005, 2002).[8]

Here is Rowe's formulation of the cosmological argument:

(1) Whatever exists is either a dependent being or an independent being.

Therefore,

(2) Either there exists an independent being or every being is dependent.

(3) It is false that every being is dependent.

Therefore,

(4) There exists an independent being.

Therefore,

(5) There exists a necessary being (1968, 280).

We will focus our attention on Rowe's defence of (1), though (3) is certainly controversial and would merit much discussion if our primary focus was on evaluating the soundness of this argument simpliciter. Consider that (1) is intended to imply that whatever exists has an explanation for its existence. This 'explanation may lie either within the nature of the thing itself or in the causal efficacy of some other being' (Rowe 1968, 282). Rowe says that the claim that 'whatever exists must have an explanation of its existence' constitutes a *strong* version of the PSR. On the other hand, the claim that 'whatever *comes* into existence must have an explanation of its existence' represents a *weak* form of the PSR. The cosmological argument, according to Rowe, utilizes the strong version of the PSR.

For the sake of discussion, let us assume that Rowe is correct that (1) implies the strong PSR, and also that (3) is true. Granting these assumptions, the evaluation of this argument now hinges on whether the strong PSR is true. One common defence of the strong PSR is to claim that it is a metaphysical assumption required to make sense of the world. The strong PSR has to be true for any type of inquiry to make sense (Rowe 1968, 285). While this hardly amounts to a proof of the PSR, defenders of it observe that it is strange to say that it is contingent. Rowe counters that it is not entirely clear that scientists need to assume that *every* event has a cause in order to conduct scientific inquiry. Science may require only the weak PSR, not the strong version (Rowe 1968, 287).

---

[8] Not only do we choose this for the sake of simplicity, but Rowe's discussion was highly influential in later work on the cosmological argument.

Though numerous versions of the PSR have been developed in connection with the cosmological argument since Rowe's article, the principle has largely fallen out of favour in recent years.[9] Interestingly, Rowe suggests that some philosophers are probably disingenuous when it comes to the PSR. While they claim to reject it for scientific or philosophical reasons, Rowe observes they might instead be worried about the theological implications of the PSR. According to Rowe, many such philosophers who explicitly reject the PSR are actually guilty of assuming it in other areas of their research. While this is a sociological claim that we cannot investigate here, our reason for highlighting it is just to say that the PSR might not be so out of fashion as some people claim.

3.2.2 The Principle of Sufficient Reason and African Traditional Religion

We now turn to ask how this argument fares on ATR. In other words, can it be employed to demonstrate that the maximal God of ATR exists? Even more carefully, the relevant question is whether, on the assumption that ATR is true, the strong version of the PSR can be endorsed. As far as we can tell, there is a dearth of work in African thought explicitly devoted to the PSR, and so it is far from clear what to say about it in this context.[10] We tentatively submit that there is reason to suppose that at least *some version of the PSR* is implicitly taken for granted by exponents of ATR. We now examine some brief textual support for this claim.

John Mbiti remarks that '[t]here are many mysteries in the universe and whenever possible people try to find an explanation for them, whether or not the explanation is final' (1975, 31). This is a sociological claim about African worldviews which, if true, is evidence that some version of the PSR is generally accepted in the African context. Kwasi Wiredu remarks:

> There is an Akan saying to the effect that if nothing had touched the palm nut branches they would not have rattled (*Se biribi ankoka papa a anka erenye kredede*). This is often quoted by writers on Akan thought as the Akan statement of universal causation. It is right as far as it goes, but there are more explicit formulations of the principle, such as one quoted by Gyekye. *Asem biara wo ne farebae*, which, literally, means everything has what brought it about. There is another formulation which, in addition to being more literal and explicit, is also more comprehensive. It says simply that everything has its explanation (*Biribiara wo nenkyerease*). (1998: 31–2)

---

[9] This seems to be a result of discoveries in quantum mechanics which seem to indicate there are events with no distinct causes (i.e., that there is genuine randomness in the universe). These details need not concern us here.

[10] This is hardly surprising given that the emergence of professional philosophy of continent was largely to devoted to ethical and political issues.

Likewise, in *Metaphysics: The Kpim of Philosophy*, Pantaleon Iroegbu suggests that the existence of things other than God is explained by the importance of being-with-others (i.e., relationality) (1995). Again, what is not important here is whether such claims are true, but rather whether they imply a version of the PSR. Finally, in *Groundwork for a New Kind of African Metaphysics: The Idea of Predeterministic Historicity*, Aribiah David Attoe argues for a kind of relational determinism where the things that exist are relationally and necessarily the result of God, again implying a version of the PSR (2022).

There is thus reason to hold that, minimally, some version of the PSR is consistent and indeed presupposed by adherents of ATR. While the Wiredu quote appears to imply the strong PSR, more work would have to be done to show whether this is more widely accepted by exponents of ATR. The results of such an investigation would impact whether a cosmological argument motivated by the PSR can be accepted on ATR. Furthermore, more recently, modified versions of the PSR have been defended in conjunction with versions of the cosmological argument and these also merit consideration from the perspective of ATR. In sum, we submit that discussion of the PSR in the context of African thought in general and ATR, in particular, is ripe for further research. While it is tempting to conclude from this discussion that the proponent of ATR can happily endorse the cosmological argument described by Rowe, in 3.2.1 we will show why this is not the case.[11]

3.2.3 The Kalām Cosmological Argument

The *Kalām* cosmological argument is a different type of cosmological argument that focuses on considerations having to do with *time*. The argument's most vigorous contemporary defender can be found in William Lane Craig, whose 1979 book, *The Kalām Cosmological Argument*, is widely thought to have revived the argument. Here is the basic version of the argument that Craig has now been defending for over four decades:

(6) Everything that begins to exist has a cause of its existence.

(7) The universe began to exist.

Therefore,

(8) The universe has a cause of its existence (1979, 63).

---

[11] Though the PSR has not been discussed in African philosophy, we do not intend to suggest that various versions of the cosmological never come into play. For example, see Attoe (2022, 27); Wiredu (1998).

Craig further argues that there is no scientific explanation for why the universe exists (because the initial conditions and the big bang are part of the universe) and that the cause must be a personal agent.

Craig defends (6) by appealing to commonsense metaphysical intuitions. He defends (7) by arguing that an actual infinity cannot exist, in addition to showing how the Big Bang Theory supports his hypothesis. These defences have been much contested in the literature, while some who endorse the general structure of the argument question whether the cause mentioned in (8) really must be personal, instead of, say, mechanical. It would be impossible to summarize the vast literature on the argument here (see Craig and Copan 2017, 2019), and we will instead press forward to examine how it should be assessed on ATR.

3.2.4 The Kalām Cosmological Argument and African Traditional Religion

It is doubtful that the proponent of ATR can straightforwardly accept the *Kalām* cosmological argument. The doctrine of creation *ex nihilo*, which says God created the universe out of nothing, is widely taken for granted in the Western tradition. Though it is probable that many Western monotheists incorrectly understand this doctrine as God creating the universe from a well of his own energy, the doctrine implies that God literally creates from nothing, and so identifying (even subconsciously) this idea with the use of energy is mistaken.[12] Of course, creation *ex nihilo* fits nicely with the *Kalām* argument because it suggests the universe came into existence at a particular time, and so on.

It is highly unlikely, however, that proponents of ATR can coherently accept (7). For according to the creation story typical of ATR, God creates the universe *ex materia*, out of pre-existing shapeless matter.[13] Regarding this understanding of creation Wiredu writes that '[i]n the most usual sense creation presupposes raw materials. A carpenter creates a chair out of wood and a novelist creates fiction out of words and ideas. [...] God is conceived as a kind of cosmic architect who fashions a world order out of indeterminate raw material' (1998, 30). On this view, God and this pre-existing matter can plausibly be understood as eternal. This means that ATR says that (7) is false. The universe was still designed by God on this view (as we will see in 3.3), but its fundamental building blocks existed prior to God's creative act. So, while it is appropriate to attribute the cause of the (alleged or apparent) structure of the universe to God, the proponent of ATR cannot say the universe itself began to exist in the sense implied by this argument. It is true that in some sense the perceived universe began to exist when God shaped

---

[12] See: ex-apologist: On Views about Creation and Their Implications (exapologist.blogspot.com)

[13] Although it should be noted that this doctrine is not universally accepted amongst Africans south of the Sahara (Wiredu 1998, 42).

and designed the universe, but the fundamental building blocks already existed. There was therefore something eternal 'before' the universe as we know it began to exist, which is not distinct from the universe.

Another problem with affirming this argument is that, on the ATR view, creation is typically understood as an ongoing event that may never end, instead of as occurring in a single big bang (Mbiti 1975, 32). Mbiti writes that '[t]he universe is considered to be unending in terms of both space and time. Nobody can reach the edge of the universe, since it has no known edge or rim' (Mbiti 1975, 34). Likewise, he adds that '[i]n terms of time, it makes sense for people to believe that there was a beginning for the universe, even though they do not know when it was. But nobody thinks that there will ever be an end to it' (Mbiti 1975, 34). If the universe did not have a starting point, then the universe is eternal (Mbiti 1975, 35).[14] It thus appears that even apart from considerations about the eternal status of the pre-existing building blocks there are reasons on ATR for holding that the universe is eternal. Cosmological arguments that rely on the claim that the universe began to exist fail if ATR is true.[15]

By way of concluding, it is worth briefly mentioning the implications that creation *ex materia* has for the doctrine of divine aseity. This doctrine says that God is wholly self-existent, self-sufficient, and completely independent.[16] Philosophers have explored whether necessary truths like 2+2=4 (and more controversially, perhaps moral laws), pose a challenge to divine aseity. For the truth of 2+2=4 does not in any way appear to *depend* on God's existence, let alone his creative work. If God did not exist, or existed but created nothing at all, it seems intuitively obvious that 2+2=4 would still be true.[17] There are a few possible solutions to this problem that we will not wade into here (e.g., Dumsday 2021; Gould 2014). Instead, consider that on the doctrine of creation *ex materia* posited by ATR, a similar problem for divine aseity emerges. This is because if the pre-existing matter God uses to create the world exists eternally, it necessarily does so apart from God. If God did not exist or if God chose instead not to mould the pre-existing matter into our universe, the pre-existing material

---

14 Interestingly, that the universe is eternal is the common view of atheists in the history of philosophy.

15 Of course, it would be inaccurate to say that all of the scholarship on ATR denies *creation ex nihilio*. For example, Mbiti writes, 'God created out of nothing, in the original act of creation, though now He may use existing materials to continue His creative activities' (1970, 51; see also Mbiti 1975, 52).

16 There is debate about whether this doctrine entails the doctrine of divine simplicity, but this is not important for our purposes.

17 Some will protest here that if God did not exist, then it is metaphysically impossible that anything else exists, so the world comparisons we are making here are nonsensical. Note that even if this is so, we can still consider these comparisons as *epistemically* possible.

would still exist by definition. The problem here is not about a necessary truth like the aforementioned mathematical case, but rather that God relied on something outside of himself in order to create the universe. If God relied on something outside of himself, then God is not entirely self-sufficient and completely independent. Thus, the ATR doctrine of creation *ex materia* poses a challenge to divine aseity.[18]

Now, worries about divine aseity will not gain very much traction for proponents of ATR who affirm the limited-God thesis. However, proponents of ATR who affirm the maximal or omni conception of God do need to grapple with this problem. One move for them, however, would be to deny that independence is in fact a great-making feature, where interdependence instead is. Consider the perspective of Desmond Tutu, the influential South African theologian, when he remarks, 'The completely self-sufficient person would be subhuman' (1999: 214). Tutu and some others in the African tradition prize, above all, certain kinds of loving relationships in which mutual aid is present. Finally, recall that in 3.2.1, we saw a cosmological argument for the conclusion that '(5) There exists a necessary being'. Notice that this argument is presumably attempting to demonstrate that there is *one* necessary being, namely, God. If there is pre-existing material that God used to create, and it necessarily exists, then ATR turns out to be inconsistent with the first cosmological argument we examined.

3.3 Creation *Ex Materia* versus Creation *Ex Nihilo*

Before moving to the teleological argument, we wish to examine one potential advantage that the doctrine of creation *ex materia* possesses over creation *ex nihilo*. This advantage has to do with God's *greatness* as exemplified in the creative process. Though the specifics as to how to spell out these attributes is hotly debated, Christianity, Islam, Judaism, and the version of ATR that affirms the maximal God all seem to agree that God is omniscient, omnipotent, and omnibenevolent. But consider that it may well take *more* power, knowledge, and creativity to form the world out of pre-existing material than to create it out of nothing. On ATR, God had to use what was already there. Retrofitting an old house with modern plumbing, electricity, heating, and so on is often more difficult than simply building a brand-new house from materials one ordered specifically for that purpose. By analogy, it is more difficult to design and build the universe out of pre-existing material than to start with nothing. This means that creation *ex materia* possibly does a better job of explaining divine attributes such as omniscience and omnipotence than creation *ex nihilo*.

---

[18] Notice that this would not be a problem for the limited-God view since God is not thought to be self-sufficient.

It is also important to recognize that though all monotheistic religions, by definition, point to the existence of one God, it is an open question whether all of the properties they each ascribe to God are compatible with one another. For Wiredu, the difference between creation *ex nihilo* and creation *ex materia* are so significant that they point to incompatible versions of God. He writes:

> Akan God is a cosmic architect while Anselm's is an ex nihilo creator. These two concepts are so different that the chances are that the ingenious saint would have considered the Akan concept quite atheistic. Accordingly, when we use the word God to translate *Nyame*, we must bear the disparity in connotation between this and the orthodox Christian concept of God firmly in mind. (Wiredu 1998, 37)

Finally, if it is metaphysically impossible to create out of nothing, then God perhaps cannot be faulted for not doing so. To challenge God's omniscience or omnipotence on such grounds is akin to complaining that God cannot square a circle, sin, or will himself out of existence. Such worries rest on category mistakes. This is one reason in itself to favour the doctrine of creation *ex materia* over the doctrine of creation *ex nihilo*. Specifically, the doctrine does not (possibly) rest on a metaphysical impossibility or at least what is incomprehensible to many of us. Consider what Wiredu says about how creation is understood by the Akans (of Ghana):

> God is the creator of the world, but he is not apart from the universe: He together with the world constitutes the spatio-temporal 'totality' of existence. In the deepest sense, therefore, the ontological chasm indicated by the natural/supernatural distinction does not exist within Akan cosmology. When God is spoken of as creator we must remind ourselves that words can mislead. Creation is often thought of, at least in run-of-the-mill Christianity, as the bringing into existence of things out of nothing. The Akan God is certainly not thought of as such a creator. The notion of creation out of nothing does not even make sense in the Akan language. (1998, 29)

Similarly, we have just seen that the African picture of creation might actually do a better job of highlighting God's greatness than does the creation story of the Abrahamic faiths. These advantages of creation *ex materia* may well outweigh the costs of any unique problems the doctrine generates for divine aseity, if indeed those are even problems.

3.4 The Teleological Argument

Teleological or Design Arguments purport to show that there is good reason to believe that (a) our universe was designed and (b) it was designed by God. Just what constitutes those 'good reasons' remains a matter of debate. In what follows we first examine William Paley's classic design argument, suggesting that it could be coherently endorsed by the follower of ATR. After that, we examine a more recent Fine-Tuning Argument, explaining that whether it can be endorsed on ATR rests on whether multiverse theories are consistent with ATR.

3.4.1 The Design Argument

While there are numerous versions of these arguments, one of the most widely known can be found in the work of William Paley. Here is the classic statement of his argument:

> [S]uppose I found a watch upon the ground, and it should be inquired how the watch happened to be in that place, I should hardly think ... that, for anything I knew, the watch might have always been there. Yet why should not this answer serve for the watch as well as for [a] stone [that happened to be lying on the ground]? ... For this reason, and for no other; namely, that, if the different parts had been differently shaped from what they are, if a different size from what they are, or placed after any other manner, or in any order than that in which they are placed, either no motion at all would have been carried on in the machine, or none which would have answered the use that is now served by it. (Paley 1867, 1)

The analogy Paley draws is between the watch and the complexity we observe in the world. Ecosystems are highly complex in addition to operations of the human body, animal bodies, flora, fauna, and so on. These highly complex systems that also have very clear functions, for example, the eye is a complex system, and its function is vision. Given the complexity of the world in conjunction with the apparent function of things in the world, we should infer that they were intelligently designed. Paley's argument has been criticized for a variety of reasons, including the fact that natural selection perfectly explains the apparent design of the phenomena Paley refers to without requiring a designer (and is thus a simpler explanation). Random genetic mutations that are passed on in a species are going to be the ones that are conducive to survival. This may well give such mutations the appearance of design if given enough time.

3.4.2 The Design Argument and African Traditional Religion

Regardless of the success or failure of Paley's design argument, the proponent of ATR is able to coherently endorse it in much the same way that those of the Abrahamic faiths can endorse it. The doctrine of creation *ex materia* does not rule out this argument. Indeed, the creation account salient in ATR perfectly fits with this argument, since on that picture God designs the universe out of pre-existing material. As mentioned in 3.3 this type of creative act is plausibly thought to be more impressive than the one of the Abrahamic faiths. In 3.4.5 we will examine reasons unique to ATR which could serve to strengthen teleological arguments.

3.4.3 The Fine-Tuning Argument

More recent versions of the design argument tend to focus on the *fine-tuning* of the universe. This is because scientists have discovered that the physical constants of the universe are such that if they were only ever so slightly different, life in the universe would be impossible. Scientists report that even a change in the degree of 10^{60} to any of these constants would make life in our universe impossible. Given the incredibly unlikely odds of our universe being life-permitting, we should infer that it was designed for life. Again, such considerations seem perfectly consistent with ATR. God had to shape the pre-existing material very precisely in order to construct a universe that is suitable for life.

The rise of multiverse theories in scientific discourse, however, has brought about a unique challenge to fine-tuning arguments. In fact, the majority of cosmologists now affirm that our universe is just one in a vast multiverse of universes. Many also hold that this vast multiverse contains innumerably many more universes than 10^{60}. This means that it might turn out not to be that unlikely that one of the universes happens to be able to support biological life. Thus, the existence of a multiverse poses a challenge to fine-tuning arguments, because, if our universe is just one among a vast multiverse of universes. Consider that if there are something like $10^{600000000}$ or more universes, it unsurprising that the physical constants in one of the universes happens to support life. We are simply lucky to find ourselves in such a universe. As Peter van Inwagen explains:

> As far as our present knowledge goes (aside from any divine revelations various individuals or groups may be privy to), we have no reason to prefer either of the following two hypotheses to the other:
>
> - This is the only cosmos [i.e., universe], and some rational being has (or rational beings have) fine-tuned it in such a way that it is a suitable abode for life.
> - This is only one among a vast number of cosmoi [i.e., universes] (some of which are – a statistical certainty – suitable abodes for life).
>
> We do not know whether the apparently purposive fine-tuning of the cosmos is reality or mere appearance, a product of chance and an observational selection effect. (2009, 202)

Whether there are resources for the monotheist to respond here remains an open question, with the most obvious route to rejecting this argument being to reject the claim that there is enough evidence to believe that we are in a multiverse (see Kraay 2015).[19]

3.4.4 The Fine-Tuning Argument and African Traditional Religion

In light of the previous discussion, in order to assess whether a fine-tuning argument could be embraced on ATR, the key question is whether multiverse theories could be accepted in this tradition. This is a place where more scholarship explicitly examining the implications of multiverse theories in the context of African cosmology is required. The various African creation stories and myths rarely (if ever) discuss the possibility of a multiverse. They typically only imply that God has created one universe and placed humans at the centre of it. Whether the creation story in ATR could be synthesized and made consistent with multiverse theories is an open question. On the one hand, if it cannot, then the proponent of ATR is free to endorse fine-tuning arguments without worrying about the potential defeater posed by the existence of the multiverse. However, on the other, this would mean that ATR must reject the idea that cosmologists *could* be right that our universe is in a multiverse. This raises questions about the relationship between religion and science in general, and the relationship between ATR and science in particular. These are topics that have yet to receive sufficiently extensive discussion in contemporary African philosophy, though a common position to encounter is that the imperceptible agency of God, ancestors, and the like often works through natural mechanisms as understood by the scientific method (e.g., Sogolo 1993; cf. Mbiti 1970: 222, 261–2). This view suggests that religious and scientific explanations should usually be consistent, with science often providing the 'how' and religion the 'why'.

3.4.5 Traditional African Ideas about Hierarchy and Interconnectedness in Relation to Design and Fine-Tuning

It is striking that there are distinct resources in ATR that can be appealed to in order to potentially bolster design and fine-tuning arguments. The hierarchy that ATR posits with God at the top, followed by ancestors, humans, non-human animals, and non-sentient nature is a hierarchy grounded in vital energy or life force. Accordingly, part of one's purpose or design is to preserve and increase the vital energy of others (and in oneself too) (see also Section 5). Furthermore, from an African worldview, it makes little sense to think of oneself as flourishing if

---

[19] It should be noted that some dispute the claims in this section and deny that the multiverse hypothesis poses a defeater to the fine-tuning argument. This is because the multiverse as a system of universes must still be governed by laws of nature that required an explanation. For more see Rees (1999).

one's broader community is not also flourishing. An individual's vitality cannot be preserved and increased in a vacuum apart from the health of one's community. Based on vital energy and the type of interconnectedness that it implies exists between individuals, we can posit two theories about its existence:

- The existence of vital energy in everything that exists, in addition to the deep interconnectedness of everything that exists, is the result of random chance.

Or

- The existence of vital energy in everything that exists, in addition to the deep interconnectedness of everything that exists, is the result of the universe being designed.

Insofar as the second explanation is more probable than the first, one could infer from features of the world uniquely posited by ATR that it was designed. But what would make it more likely to be designed than random chance? Following Paley, a first step might be to observe the high degree of complexity involved in such interconnectedness, with the further argument that such complexity is unlikely to be the result of random processes.[20] Admittedly, more steps are required to get from there to the claim that God exists, but we submit that this is the beginning of a novel design argument. The Westerner may perhaps be quick to object that she does not believe in vital energy, or the type of interconnectedness described here. But notice this is not what is at stake in this argument. The argument in question assumes that vital energy exists and instead focuses on what best explains its existence. Plus, it could be that another version of the argument is available, with somewhat less contested premises to the effect that everything is made of the same basic stuff (whether vital energy or something purely physical) and richly interconnected (consider non-locality in quantum mechanics). Those premises also point towards a single artist. We believe these suggestions point to future avenues for fruitful research.

3.5 Conclusion

In this section, we have examined two different versions of each of the cosmological and teleological arguments. It is tempting to conclude that the cosmological argument that rests on the PSR might be consistent with ATR since the relevant form of the PSR is consistent with it. The *Kalām* Cosmological Argument is more straightforwardly incompatible with ATR since it rejects the doctrine of creation *ex nihilo*. We also observed that while the ATR doctrine

---

[20] Likewise, if the interconnectedness were not conducive to fitness, then this would also perhaps be a reason to think it was not the result of chance.

of creation *ex materia* might pose a unique challenge to divine aseity, it plausibly does a better job of explaining God's power and creative work than creation *ex nihilo*. It also shows why it is easy for the proponent of ATR to endorse classical design arguments for God's existence. Whether it is also consistent with more recent fine-tuning arguments remains to be seen because such consistency hinges on whether multiverse theories are compatible with ATR.

We noted throughout this section a number of additional places for fruitful dialogue between the Anglo-American philosophy of religion and African philosophy of religion. Not only are there many more formulations of each of the arguments we discussed, but also there are many more arguments for the existence of God that we have not mentioned at all. To name a few, such arguments include those from meaning, morality, religious experience, Pascal's wager, and the ontological argument. We conclude that there is much work to be done in analysing arguments for the existence of God from the perspective of ATR.

4 Arguments Against the Existence of God

4.1 Introduction

This section examines three arguments against the existence of God as found in the problem of divine hiddenness, the problem of no best world, and the evidential problem of evil. This section suggests that there are unique and previously unexplored responses to the problem of divine hiddenness when examined from ATR. For example, on ATR God is typically thought to be quite distant from humans because God is so wholly different. Divine hiddenness is less of a surprise on ATR than on more Western conceptions of monotheism. The problem of no best world says that for any world God creates, there is a better world that God could have created. God's creative work is therefore always morally surpassable, something that is supposed to be impossible on perfect being theism. We will show that whether there are ways out of this problem on ATR may well rest on whether the view is consistent with our universe being in a multiverse. With respect to the problem of evil, this section cross-examines responses to it found in both ATR and the Anglo-American tradition, with a particular focus on areas for future research.

4.2 The Problem of Divine Hiddenness

Though we find statements complaining of God's hiddenness throughout the history of philosophy (and literature), the idea was not really leveraged into an explicit argument for atheism until J.L. Schellenberg's groundbreaking book, *Divine Hiddenness and Human Reason* (1993). Schellenberg remains the foremost defender of the argument and his work is largely the focal point of the literature (see Kraay 2013).

4.2.1 Schellenberg's Argument

Here is a straightforward version of Schellenberg's argument:

(1) If a perfectly loving God exists, then there exists a God who is always open to a personal relationship with any finite person (Schellenberg 2015, 38).

(2) If there exists a God who is always open to a personal relationship with any finite person, then no finite person is ever nonresistantly in a state of nonbelief in relation to the proposition that God exists (Schellenberg 2015, 53).

(3) Some finite persons are or have been nonresistantly in a state of nonbelief in relation to the proposition that God exists (Schellenberg 2015, 74).

Therefore,

(4) God does not exist.

Briefly, here is some motivation for the premises. With respect to (1), Schellenberg focuses on the idea that if God exists, then a relationship with God is one of the greatest possible goods. Since it is such a great good and God is all-loving, God will *always* be open to such relationships. In light of this fact, (2) says that if God exists, there will not be any nonresistant nonbelief, which means that we can also add that the nonresistant belief is nonculpable. A relationship with God is so valuable that people would not be unable to have such a relationship through no fault of their own. However, (3) contends that there are in fact people who fail to believe that God exists through no fault of their own. This premise can be motivated by reflecting on the following question: Is it more obvious that there are such individuals who exist or that God exists? The former is more obvious than the latter because it appears that there are people who genuinely pursue God, desperately seek out a relationship with him, and yet fail to believe that God exists. The fact that such individuals exist demonstrates (4), that God doesn't exist. If God existed, he would ensure that those genuinely open to him would have a relationship with him.

This argument has been challenged in many different ways, and a full summary of the responses in the literature is impossible here. Some responses include the idea that the relevant type of nonbelief simply does not occur, that belief is not a necessary condition for a relationship with God, that God hiding ensures people are free to choose him, and that God hiding is an act of mercy (e.g., Cullison 2010; Dumsday 2012; Hernry 2001).

4.2.2 The Problem of Divine Hiddenness and African Traditional Religion

One of the keys to success for Schellenberg's hiddenness argument is that God is *always* open to a relationship to finite beings such as humans. But Schellenberg's argument focuses on the Judeo-Christian understanding of God. Indeed, the vast majority of theologians and philosophers he cites to demonstrate (i) that God is open to a relationship with humans and (ii) that such a relationship is incredibly valuable are working within a Judeo-Christian tradition. Of course, Schellenberg ought not to be faulted for working within a particular tradition. However, if what he says is supposed to generalize to *any* conception of monotheism that holds God is omniscient, omnibenevolent, and omnipotent, then there is a problem here. For (1) is false according to ATR. Before explaining in further detail why this is the case, notice that the proponent of the hiddenness argument could simply block our move and maintain that the hiddenness argument applies only to the God of the Judeo-Christian tradition. However, even if this move is legitimate, it would still be interesting to know *why* the argument does not apply to ATR.

(1) is false on ATR because, according to much of this tradition, it is false that God is always open to a personal relationship with every finite person. Consider the following statements about the distance of God from exponents of ATR:

> Informants do not talk about the 'withdrawal' of the Supreme Being. He has never been near, and there is no question of his having been pushed aside by other divine forms more responsive to their needs. The elders insist that his passivity is not their punishment for his relegation: things have always been like that, and people have not suffered as a result. (Ubah 1982, 92)

> The universe is a chain of forces 'empowering' and 'depowering' each other. God is the universal superforce, charging everything. God has important business, so he does not deal with humans directly. He leaves this to others: the young go to the elders, the elders to the ancestors, and to the diviner, who is in contact not only with the ancestors, but also with powerful spirits, people who died and whom we know only as a force (Hamminga 2005 63).

> ATR conceives God as so great and majestic that he cannot deal directly with puny mortals without humans suffering the harm of direct encounter with divine majesty (cf. Paris (1995), 30). Achebe (1994, 180) reconciles the notion of God's hiddenness and the idea of his transcendence in ATR with his master–servant analogy, where God is the master and lesser deities are his servants who must serve as intermediaries given the privileged standing of the master. God's remoteness, Achebe notes, does not stop the Igbo from describing him with the name Chukwuka, which means 'Chukwu [God] is Supreme' (Achebe 1994, 180) (Agada 2022a, 3).

These passages suggest that exponents of ATR will doubt there is a sufficient reason for God to offer a relationship to us. At the very least, ATR values or expects such a relationship significantly less than in the Abrahamic faiths. On ATR, God's wishes are mediated through the invisible realm, and most commonly through departed ancestors. Significant distance between God and humans (i.e., finite or at least even more limited and perceptible creatures) is inbuilt by the hierarchical nature of the world as posited on ATR.[21]

This distance between God and humans is unsurprising on ATR because God is so wholly other. Since God is such an altogether different being from humans, it is unsurprising that God remains mostly hidden from us. There is an interesting connection between this idea and a branch of Western thought known as *negative theology*. This school of theology claims that because God is so different from us, we cannot make positive knowledge claims about God's nature. At best, we can perhaps make statements only about what God is not. We are bound by our finitude to describe God's nature with analogies to ungodlike things.

One fascinating anthropological observation in this context is that despite ATR predicting a very hidden God, atheism is virtually non-existent in traditional African societies. This is surely not to say that no Africans are living on the continent today who are not atheists. As many African societies become more urbanized, diverse, and Westernized, rates of atheism on the continent have been on the rise in recent years. The point is that in traditional societies where ATR flourished (untouched by colonial influences), atheism does not appear to have existed at least not to a noticeable degree. The anthropological point we are making is that belief in God's existence flourishes in such societies even in the face of God's hiddenness. Since God's hiddenness is posited by ATR, the believer may well be less bothered by their experience of divine hiddenness. That they also have clear alternatives to direct communion with God in the form of, say, interaction with departed ancestors may also serve to mitigate worries about divine hiddenness. On ATR there appear to be more options to have a relationship with God mediated through other beings than there are to be found in the Abrahamic faiths. In sum, divine hiddenness is a feature of ATR, not a bug.

4.3 The Problem of No Best World

The problem of no best world is the only *a priori* argument for God's non-existence that has received significant attention in the contemporary Anglo-American philosophy of religion.[22] Instead of focusing on particular

---

[21] It should be noted that at least some African creation myths state that God was not always as hidden as he is now. The sin of humans occasioned God to eventually withdraw from them.

[22] Indeed, it is the only *a priori* argument for God's non-existence of which we are aware, apart from claims that the concept of God is logically contradictory.

facts about the actual world (e.g., evil or divine hiddenness), the problem comes in the form of a dilemma suggesting that no matter what type of world we inhabit, God could not have created it.

4.3.1 Rowe's Problem

The problem of no best world came to prominence with the publication of William Rowe's book, *Can God Be Free?* (2004). Rowe formulates the argument as an unpalatable dilemma for the monotheist:

(5) God can either create the best possible world or create a less-than-best world.

(6) If there is a best world, then God must create it.

(7) If God must create the best possible world, then God is not free.

(8) If there is no best world, then God can only create a less-than-best world.

(9) If God creates a less-than-best world, then God's work is morally surpassable.

(10) Either God is not free, or God's work is morally surpassable.

Therefore,

(11) God does not exist.

The upshot here is that no matter which type of world we are in, God could not have created it. Let's briefly motivate each of these premises. With respect to (5), there is either a best world or there is not a best world. God has only two options with respect to divine creation. Some have countered that there might be multiple best worlds (perhaps based on the fact that some great-making properties of worlds are incommensurate with each other). However, if this is the case, then God's choice to create one of the best worlds is arbitrary. Alternatively, if God must create all these worlds, then God's act of creation is still not free. So, we will set aside the option of multiple best worlds.

(6) says if there is a best world, then God must create it. If God failed to choose the best world when it was an option, he would be choosing the less-than-best. This runs counter to perfect being theology in serious ways.[23] However, (7), if the existence of a best world means that God *must* create it, then God is not free. This is problematic because the Abrahamic faiths typically maintain that God has

---

[23] Leibniz motivated this something like (6) using the *Principle of the Best* and the *Principle of Sufficient Reason*.

libertarian freedom (or something close to it). On the other hand, if there is no best world, then (8) follows as a matter of definition. For there would only be less than best worlds that God could create. The problem with this option is that this would make (9) true. Any world God created would be morally surpassable. Notice that this premise is not requiring that God do something logically impossible. The premise does not rest on the idea that God cannot create the best possible world, which would be impossible if there was no best world. Rather, it rests on the fact that for any world God creates in this scenario, his work is necessarily morally surpassable. There is always a better world that he could have created. These premises lead us to the two horns of the dilemma in (10). The reason that they entail (11), that God does not exist, is fairly straightforward. According to Rowe, if God is not free then a radical revisioning of perfect being theology is required. It might still be true that there is a supernatural being, but our conception of it would be so entirely different that it would be inappropriate to label it 'God'. It is just as problematic if God's work turns out to be morally surpassable. If an unsurpassable being creates something, we would not expect it to be surpassable. In particular, we would not expect that anything he created would be morally surpassable. Either option leads to a serious challenge to the existence of God.

This problem has generated a significant amount of attention in contemporary philosophy of religion. Robert Adams argues that even if there is a best possible world, that God would not be obligated to create it, though this contention has hardly been met with universal praise (1972). Others have suggested that if we are in a 'no best world scenario' God is morally permitted to create a world at random (above some threshold) (Howard-Snyder and Howard-Snyder 1994; Penner 2006).

4.3.2 The Problem of No Best World and African Traditional Religion

In 2.4.3 we noted that whether an objection to the teleological argument applies in the context of ATR rests on whether multiverse theories are plausible on ATR. While, if accepted, the multiverse might lead the adherent of ATR to lose the teleological argument, here the multiverse provides a potential solution to the Problem of No Best World. Klaas J. Kraay argues that God created the best possible world that contains all the universes worthy of creation (2011). This idea nicely captures the strong intuition that given the evil in our particular world (i.e., our universe) it could not possibly be the best, in addition to the intuition that God's creative work cannot be morally surpassable. Thus, if the proponent of ATR can endorse a multiverse, an additional resource is available to them to help avoid the problem of no best world.

In order to address the problem of no best world from the perspective of ATR more directly, we need to know more about how it understands divine creation. In 2.3 we saw that according to ATR, God creates *ex materia* and more generally is limited for some versions of ATR. It does not appear that Rowe's reasoning applies to a limited God that is not, say, omniscient and omnipotent.

But just what sort of world would an omni-God (or something close to it) create, morally speaking, for the African tradition? While discussing the problem of evil in ATR, Wiredu makes an observation about his Ghanaian people that is relevant here:

> The Akans delight in crediting their maxims to animals, and in this instance the epigrammatic surrogate is the hawk. It is said: 'The hawk says that all that God created is good' (*Osansa se nea Onyame yee biara ye*). The sense here is not that all is good to a degree that could conceivably be exceeded but rather that all is maximally good. Again, the hawk is not trying to fly in the face of the palpable facts of evil in the world; what it is saying is that the evil, though it is evil, is unavoidably involved in the good and is ultimately for the best-a sentiment that would have warmed the heart of Leibniz, author, in Western philosophy, of the maxim that this is the best of all possible worlds (1998, 40–1).

At least within the indigenous Akan worldview, then, there appears to be support for the claim that God does indeed create the best possible world. As far as we can tell, the question of whether God can be libertarian free if he creates the best world has not been discussed extensively in the context of ATR. According to Wiredu, the Akan position coincides with the view that good cannot exist without evil. It is reminiscent of Leibniz's painting analogy. When one looks closely at a painting it might appear quite ugly. However, when one steps back to observe the whole, they recognize that the ugly part contributes to the overall beauty of the painting (see *Theodicy* [1709] (1952)).

This discussion leads nicely into our final topic of the section, the problem of evil. For even supposing that Rowe is wrong, and there is no challenge to theism if God creates in a 'best world scenario' or 'no best world scenario', the problem of evil remains. Suppose that in a 'no best world scenario' since there is no best world for God to create, he is free to choose a sufficiently good enough world for creation. Even setting aside Rowe's challenge that this implies that God's creative work is morally surpassable, we can still rightly wonder whether our world really is sufficiently good enough for a creation given all the evil, that is, non-instrumental badness that exists within it. Alternatively, if there is a best world and God creates it, setting aside Rowe's contention that this denies divine freedom, the problem remains. For how can our world which contains so much evil possibly be the best world? The next section takes up the problem of evil in the context of ATR.

4.4 The Problem of Evil

If the problem of evil is not the most serious challenge to the existence of God, it is certainly the longest-standing and most extensively discussed problem. Perhaps more than with any other argument in philosophical (a)theology it is misleading to speak of *the* problem of evil as if there is a unified way the problem is typically presented. In the contemporary Anglo-American philosophy of religion, there are two main versions of the argument as found in the *logical problem of evil* and the *evidential problem of evil*. The former argument seeks to establish the strong claim that God's existence is *logically incompatible* with the existence of any evil (see Mackie 1982; Plantinga 1989).[24] If God's existence makes the existence of evil impossible, then even just one instance of evil in our world entails God's non-existence. We say this argument relies on a strong claim because it implies that there is no logically possible reason why God might permit evil.[25] In light of this, we will instead focus on the widely discussed evidential problem of evil, which is probabilistic.

4.4.1 The Evidential Problem of Evil

The evidential problem of evil takes on a variety of different forms. In its most basic, it focuses on the idea that the quality and/or quantity of evil found in the world makes it less likely that God exists. The focus of such formulations is often on the apparent existence of gratuitous evil. Here is the formulation of the argument we will work with:

(12) If God exists, then there should be no instances of gratuitous evil.

(13) Probably, there are instances of gratuitous evil.

Therefore,

(14) Probably, God doesn't exist.

When we parse the terms 'God' and 'gratuitous', premise (12) is supposed to be intuitively obvious. If God is all-knowing, all-good, and all-powerful, he would not permit instances of gratuitous evil. An evil is typically thought to be gratuitous if its occurrence does not prevent an otherwise worse evil from occurring or lead to an otherwise unobtainable greater good. In other words, an all-loving God would not want there to be any pointless evils. His knowledge would allow him to identify

---

[24] For discussion of this problem in African philosophy of religion see Cordeiro-Rodrigues and Chimakonam (2022); Chimakonam and Chimakonam (2022).

[25] Though there was a period where it was widely thought Alvin Plantinga (1989) had solved the logical problem of evil, in recent years this consensus has crumbled (e.g., Almeida 2012, Schellenberg 2013)

such evils and his power would allow him to prevent them from occurring. While (12) is usually not the main point of contention, it is noteworthy that some theists explicitly deny that God's existence is incompatible with gratuitous evil (e.g., Hasker 1992; van Inwagen 2006). The debate over this and related arguments most often focuses on the truth of (13). Another way of thinking about what is at stake here is in the form of the following question: Is it more likely that God exists or that there are instances of gratuitous evil? Defenders of this argument have been quick to point to numerous real-world examples of evils that they maintain the theist will be hard-pressed to deny are gratuitous. Rowe's suffering fawn is one of the most oft referred to of such examples:

> Suppose in some distant forest lightning strikes a dead tree, resulting in a forest fire. In the fire a fawn is trapped, horribly burned, and lies in terrible agony for several days before death relieves its suffering. So far as we can see, the fawn's intense suffering is pointless. For there does not appear to be any greater good such that the prevention of the fawn's suffering would require either the loss of that good or the occurrence of an evil equally bad or worse. Nor does there seem to be any equally bad or worse evil so connected to the fawn's suffering that it would have had to occur had the fawn's suffering been prevented. Could an omnipotent, omniscient being have prevented the fawn's apparently pointless suffering? The answer is obvious, as even the theist will insist. An omnipotent, omniscient being could have easily prevented the fawn from being horribly burned, or, given the burning, could have spared the fawn the intense suffering by quickly ending its life, rather than allowing the fawn to lie in terrible agony for several days. (1979, 337)

Consider that somewhere between 500 million and 1 billion animals died in the Australian wildfires of 2019. In what follows, we will first explore some potential responses found in the African tradition before turning to the Anglo-American tradition. The problem of evil has likely received the most attention in the African philosophy of religion of any of the arguments we discuss in this Element.

4.4.2 African Responses to the Problem of Evil

Determinism/Fate

One type of response to the evidential problem of evil that does not feature in the contemporary Anglo-American literature is based on appeals to fate. However, fate appears in the African literature implying that both the good and bad found in a person's life are determined.[26] If a person's life is fated, then the evil they experience is perhaps an unavoidable feature of their life, an inescapable part of the universe, and hence not gratuitous. Kwame Gyekye (1995) says that the notion

---

[26] Of course, this is not to say that the idea of fate has not featured prominently at various points in Western thought.

of fate can be found in Akan thought given that everyone is assigned a fate prior to their birth (see also Paris 1995, 108). Luis Cordeiro-Rodrigues and Ada Agada explain that 'Gyekye's stance is a soft determinism position since he asserts that God only determines the broad outlines of a person's life, not the minute detail' (2022, 8).

Notice that though fate may well explain why an individual experiences suffering, it does not explain where fates come from or who assigns them. Positing the existence of fates containing evil in a world created by God does not explain why such fates are co-possible with God in the first place.[27] Another important question is the degree to which fates are, if at all, completely fixed or changeable. If a bad fate can to some extent be changed, then it is plausible some responsibility for the evil in a fate could be shifted away from God and placed on humans. Peter J. Paris writes:

> in contrast to those who are born with good destinies, it is widely believed that some people are bearers of various types of bad destinies. Some of them are capable of modifications; others not. In either case, with the combined help of professional diviners and much concentrated effort on their own part, humans may, to a certain extent, overcome many aspects of a bad destiny. Thus the notion of destiny, whether good or bad, does not imply human passivity. Instead it informs persons about the possibilities that they are either capable or incapable of realizing. (1995, 132)

Perhaps the inability to avoid a bad fate would contribute to an overall harmony amongst forces in the universe, while the ability to avoid a bad fate would place responsibility for it on one's shoulders. However, it remains difficult to see how either consideration would account for Rowe's suffering fawn.

God Can Do Evil

Though well known for his efforts towards decolonizing African philosophy of religion, John A.I. Bewaji actually does seem to affirm the maximal conception of God (though this is admittedly not always clear in his writings). For example, he writes that 'Olodumare is the Most Powerful Being for Whom Nothing is too Great or too Small, Below or Beyond Accomplish [and] Olodumare's Knowledge is Incomparable and Hence Has no Equal' (Bewaji 1998, 8). Instead, Bewaji answers the problem of evil in a way that many working in the Anglo-American tradition focused on the Abrahamic faiths will find quite surprising. He contends that God can do evil because to deny this is possible is

---

[27] Though some African scholars claim God always assigns a good fate, while perhaps malevolent spiritual entities assign bad fates, this would not change the basic point. It could still be asked why God permits malevolent entities to assign people bad fates.

to put a limitation on God's power. Bewaji claims that '[t]here is no doubt that God is the most powerful Being and that He has all the superlative attributes one can consider, but the Yoruba do not think that such a being cannot do evil or cause evil. It is part of the attributes of the Supreme Being to be able to utilize all things' (Bewaji 1998, 11; see also Bewaji 1988, 243). He later adds that 'to say that God does not or cannot do evil is to unnecessarily circumscribe His power [and] God is the most powerful Being, hence, He does and can do anything, including good and evil' (Bewaji 1998, 11).

Though this is clearly a minority view, Bewaji is not alone in it with, for example, G.S. Sogolo (1993, 14) appears to agree with it and A.K. Fayemi writing that '[t]he problem of evil does not therefore exist in Yoruba thought because *Olodumare* and his divinities are said to be capable of doing both good and bad' (2012, 11).[28] While this solution to the problem of evil seems straightforwardly at odds with the maximal conception of God associated with the Abrahamic faiths, it has not received systematic evaluation in the Anglo-American tradition, which tends to assume that God is impeccable, unable to do wrong.

The Devil in African Traditional Religion

Though the devil is clearly part of the Abrahamic faiths, it is very rarely appealed to in the Anglo-American philosophical tradition, even by those writers who are members of such faiths.[29] An interesting feature of some of the African literature is that authors appear more willing to sometimes attribute the existence of evil to, if not the devil, then analogous characters. For example, in the Yoruba tradition, Adelumo P. Dopamu's book *Èṣù, the Invisible Foe of Man* (1986) argues that Esu is a close equivalent to the Western conception of the devil. However, it should be noted that this interpretation of ATR has not gone uncontested, with multiple scholars rejecting the idea that there are analogous characters to the devil in African traditions (e.g., Agada 2022b, 15; Bewaji 1998, 13; Ofuasia 2022). It would be a worthwhile project to compare and contrast the sparse literature in the Anglo-American tradition that appeals to the devil with the more robust treatments found in the contemporary ATR literature.[30]

---

[28] For other examples see Chimakonam (2022). Cordeiro-Rodrigues argues that in the context of the limited-God thesis, the Kongolese tradition doesn't claim God can do evil because he is all-powerful but simply because he is not all-good (2022). For a critical discussion of Bewaji's and Fayemi's view of God see Agada (2022b).

[29] Consider that in a *109-page* living bibliography on the problem of evil in the Anglo-American tradition since the 1950s (created and maintained by Justin Mooney), that the terms 'Satan' and 'Devil' only appear a combined 15-times. Likewise, there are only five entries under the category of 'Demonic Theodices. See Problem of Evil: Bibliography– Google Docs.

[30] For some of the rare examples of the devil in work on the problem of evil in the Anglo-American tradition see Boyd (2001); Dunnington (2018); Guthrie (2017); Martin (1983); Kelly (1997).

The Problem Still Arises on the Limited-God Thesis

As we explained in 2.8, some exponents of ATR reject the idea that '[t]here exists a Supreme Being that is omnipotent, omniscient, and omnibenevolent [and instead assert that] there is no transcendent God but only a limited deity that cannot eliminate evil in the world' (Agada 2022a, 1). Many suggest that if God is not maximal, then the problem of evil evaporates. However, Agada argues that this is mistaken because, even on the limited-God thesis, questions about evil can arise. In particular, proponents of the limited-God thesis tend to affirm that God is powerful enough to create the world out of pre-existing matter. Such a feat of strength surely implies that God could do *something* to limit the evil in the world, even if he lacks the power to eliminate it completely (Agada 2022a, 6–8, 15).[31] For instance, if God made the fawn and the forest, God could have rescued Rowe's fawn from the fire. Thus, while we are primarily concerned with the maximal conception of God in this Element, a problem of evil still exists on the limited-God thesis. Therefore, further cross-cultural philosophical dialogue regarding the problem of evil between the Anglo-American tradition and the African tradition should take place, even by those who affirm the limited-God thesis.[32]

4.4.3 Anglo-American Responses to the Evidential Problem of Evil

Freewill Defences

Perhaps the best-known response to the problem of evil is the freewill defence. This defence involves appealing to libertarian freewill as the justification for evil. God endowed humans with freewill because it is such a great good, even though it comes with the risk of humans using it for ill. Part of what makes freewill so valuable is that it is thought to be a necessary condition for morality. In order for humans genuinely to merit praise and blame for their actions, they must have libertarian freewill. In addition, it is more valuable if someone freely chooses the good, including to realize God's purpose, than if they are causally determined to do the good. Furthermore, freewill is often thought to be a necessary condition to enter into a loving relationship with God and other humans. If God didn't endow us with freewill, then humans would not be able to freely choose to enter into a relationship with him.[33]

---

[31] Agada's own fascinating view is that the pre-existing matter is vital force that exists externally from God and contains (perhaps the potential) for both good and evil. God creates the world out of this energy, displaying great power and working through humans to reduce the amount of evil (2022a, 13–14).

[32] Questions about the permissibility of *gratuitous* often appear in the Anglo-American tradition while the African tradition does not as often distinguish between gratuitous and justified evils. This is another area for further exploration.

[33] This has also been used as a response to the problem of divine hiddenness.

What does ATR say about freewill? Wiredu observes that Kwame Gyekye appeals to freewill in offering an Akan solution to the problem of evil. He says that 'Evil, according to them [i.e., the Akans], is the result of the exercise by humans of their freedom of the will with which they were endowed by the Creator, *Oboadee*' (Wiredu 1998, 39).[34] Wiredu notes that even if this response is successful, it applies only to human-caused evil. According to Wiredu, it does nothing to solve the problem of natural evil as it fails to explain the suffering caused by natural disasters like hurricanes, floods, tsunamis, and earthquakes (1998, 40). Rowe's suffering fawn seems as yet unexplained.

However, consider that the Christian tradition may be able to explain natural evil by appealing to freewill. On the Christian view, the world was originally perfect but became fallen and broken through the free choices of Adam and Eve; that is, they freely ate the forbidden fruit in the garden of Eden. The result here is not just that humans fell into sin, but that the *entire world* became fallen. This includes the natural world, and so natural evil is still ultimately the result of human freewill. Wiredu might have been too quick in thinking freewill cannot also be appealed to on ATR to explain natural evil. For instance, he quotes Helaine Minkus' 'Causal Theory in Akwapim Akan Philosophy' as claiming that the problem of evil does not arise in certain indigenous African societies because:

> God's attribute of transcendence and the concomitant belief that he has delegated power to the other agents that more directly interact with human beings pragmatically diminish His omnipotence. The other agents are treated in practice as if endowed with an independent ability to act . . . The postulation of a great number of beings empowered to affect events, joined with the acceptance of evil as necessarily co-existing with good from creation obviates the problem of evil so burdensome to those monotheistic theologians who define the Supreme Being as both omnipotent and totally benevolent and attempt a reconciliation of these qualities with the existence of evil. (Minkus quoted in Wiredu 1998, 39)

Though Wiredu contends that God is still ultimately responsible for evil on this view, it is unclear if one could lay this charge against a maximal version of God any more than it could be laid against the God of Western monotheism. God might be responsible for Adam and Eve's fall inasmuch as he endowed them with freewill and created the conditions under which they might sin. The same is true for the agents in the spiritual realm of ATR that God endows with freewill. Consider that Mbiti writes:

> We may answer this question together with another one which asks whether spirits are evil or good, malevolent or benevolent. In fact, the majority of the spirits cannot be classified as either good or bad. Whether they are felt as good

---

[34] See also Gyekye (1987).

or bad depends on how people experience the forces of nature (in effect the nature spirits) and how they act towards human beings. The spirits can do both good and evil to people, just as people do both good and evil to their fellow human beings. (1975, 73)

In both cases, though God creates the conditions under which agents *might* freely choose the bad, God is not thought to be *morally* responsible for the free decision of such agents.

That said, the rationale for how human evil is responsible for natural evil needs to be plausible, not merely valid in the sense of entailing a favoured conclusion. How could a human being making a free decision to eat from the Tree of Knowledge impair an entire physical universe? Why would not God allow this free decision to take place, but prevent some of the worst results to innocent parties, such as the suffering fawn, downstream?

Related to the issue of freewill is the nature of divine foreknowledge, which has been the subject of vigorous debate in the Anglo-American tradition (primarily between Molonists and open theists). Thus far, the literature in ATR has not substantially engaged with issues of divine foreknowledge, thereby pointing to another potential area for productive exchange with the Anglo-American literature.

Soul-Making Theodicies

Soul-making theodicies rest on the idea that when someone experiences what appears to be a gratuitous evil, it is for the greater good of developing their character. The world has been designed by God in such a way that people have freewill to choose the good but will experience suffering and temptation. While this can appear gratuitous, it is all to the end of appropriately developing their soul (e.g., Hick 1978; Stump 1993). Such evils are justified by the greater good of spiritual formation, which leads to an eternal afterlife in the presence of God. In other words, there is a spiritual dimension to evil and suffering that cannot be overlooked in discussions of whether it is justified.

It is unclear whether there are close analogues to this reasoning in ATR. Though one prominent branch of contemporary African ethics focuses on normative personhood, which is centrally about character development, it is uncertain whether it grounds close analogues to this theodicy in ATR. The work on normative personhood is decidedly secular and does not typically equate personhood with a spiritual entity such as a soul. Perhaps the closest analogue to be found is in ATR's affirmation of vital energy, where part of the goal of morality is to preserve and protect that energy. However, even this analogy is problematic as experiencing suffering and evil are typically thought to be things that weaken a person's vital energy or, indeed, consist of its weakening. That said, it appears open to the African religionist to maintain that personhood substantially comes from responding to the pain and other evils that face others. Beneficence is widely taken to be the central virtue of the tradition (e.g., Paris 1995, 136). Although it is rare to encounter the suggestion that God would allow evils to occur to some in order to facilitate personhood for others, perhaps that is implicit in the idea that good and evil are both essential for the requisite amount or kind of harmony.

Sceptical Theism

Sceptical theism is a popular response to the evidential problem of evil designed to block the inference from the observation of some evil to the claim that it is gratuitous. In one of the early motivations of this view, Stephen Wykstra defends the following principle:

> CORNEA: On the basis of cognized situation s, human H is entitled to claim 'It appears that p' only if it is reasonable for H to believe that, given her cognitive faculties and the use she has made of them, if p were not the case, s would likely be different than it is in some way discernible by her. (Wykstra 1984, 85)

CORNEA stands for 'conditions of reasonable epistemic access'. Wykstra is pressing on the idea that, given the great gulf that exists between humans and God, we ought to recognize that we probably are not in a very good epistemic position to discern whether an instance of evil is gratuitous. The literature on sceptical theism (and related epistemic principles) is now enormous, with the view enjoying great popularity amongst Anglo-American theistic philosophers of religion (for more see Dougherty 2016; Dougherty and McBrayer 2016).

In the context of the Abrahamic faiths, we have remained puzzled by sceptical theism's popularity. If the Abrahamic God exists, it seems like there are strong reasons to think we would in fact be in a good position to identify whether some instance of evil is gratuitous. However, instead of examining our objections to sceptical theism in its current context, we want to ask how it would be received on ATR. Here we think that some of the considerations that help ATR respond to the problem of divine hiddenness can also be applied in order to justify sceptical theism. Recall that according to ATR God is quite distant and withdrawn from humans; God is thought not to have provided a text or prophet to guide us, and indeed not to have communicated with us at all. It is less surprising on this view that we would not be in a good position to identify whether some evil is in fact gratuitous. In general, we have less reason to think we would be able to identify God's reasons for anything on ATR than on Western monotheism. At best, God would need to convey his moral will to ancestors, who then convey it to diviners who have alone been specially trained to receive messages from them, who in turn convey the messages to the mass of us, who finally are tasked with teaching the next generation. Perhaps the risks of the messages not being properly taught or transmitted are indeed great given the number of steps involved in transmission.

Furthermore, there is some evidence that at least some exponents of ATR would endorse principles similar to the ones affirmed by sceptical theists. Consider:

> Against the contention that an omnipotent God would not have created the world in a way that makes physical evil possible, the theistic scholar Njoku suggests that God permitted natural evil for reasons beyond human comprehension. With specific reference to Igbo cosmology, he notes: For the Igbo, to be existent in the way God is, is to be involved practically and realistically: to answer petitions and to say that He [*sic*] is around whenever, wherever and in whatever circumstances. If *Chukwu* does not answer accordingly, He is queried whether He is asleep. However 'Chukwu', 'Chineke' is a wonderful God – 'Itunuanya' – and not fully comprehensible. Humans know God in an … obscure way. (Njoku 2002, 147 quoted in Cordeiro-Rodrigues and Agada 2022, 8)

And:

> His [i.e., God's] attributes do not preclude the device and use of evil for the betterment of society. God is the creator. He created everything, both positive and negative. Why? *We cannot know. His ways are incomprehensible.* God is the most powerful Being, hence, He does and can do anything, including good and evil. (Bewaji 1998, 11; emphasis mine)

We tentatively suggest this as evidence that some proponents of ATR would embrace sceptical theism, with more work being required to spell out cross-cultural implications.

4.5 Conclusion

This section surveyed three prominent arguments for atheism in the problem of divine hiddenness, the problem of no best world, and the problem of evil. The reality of divine hiddenness may well be greater on ATR because God is thought to be more distant and separated from humans than as he is typically described by the Abrahamic faiths, which means that for ATR hiddenness is to be expected from God and not a reason to doubt God's existence. Some versions of ATR appear to affirm that God creates the best possible world, lacking a readymade answer to the problem of no best world, while other versions maintain that a limited God cannot create the best. Finally, we explored a number of both African and Anglo-American possible solutions to the problem of evil, noting that there is ample room for cross-pollination between the traditions on these topics.

5 African Religious Ethics

5.1 Introduction

In this section, we offer an account of African religious ethics. The section emerges in the light of the previous sections where we have been offering an account of ATR's relationship to important arguments and ideas found in the contemporary Anglo-American philosophy of religion. The question that arises immediately is whether such a metaphysical or religious system embodies its own ethical vision and how would it compare to the familiar ones in the Anglo-American literature like the influential Judeo-Christian ethical system of the Divine Command Theory (henceforth, DCT) or one grounded on *imago dei* (Joyce 2012). The section answers this question in the affirmative and aims to provide a picture of African religious ethics associated with our interpretation of ATR. We will construct our picture of African religious ethics by appealing to the highly prized divine or spiritual property of life force, vitality, or vital energy.

After explaining some preliminaries about the scope of our project in this section, we will discuss in more detail than the first section the ontological system associated with the concept of vitality, namely: metaphysical monism, metaphysical holism, and the function of vitality in this metaphysical system. After that we turn to the vitality-based metaethical account of moral properties before examining human dignity based on vitality and its possible contribution to bioethics. Along the way, we will point to areas for further cross-cultural dialogue with the Anglo-American religious-philosophical tradition.

5.2 African Traditional Religion and Religious Ethics

We begin by noting four clarifications in relation to our attempt to construct a picture of African religious ethics. First, this project is important because it will repudiate voices in African philosophy that have insisted that as much as there is a pervasive belief in the supreme being, God; there is also a pervasive belief that ethics is entirely secular (Wiredu 1992). At best, if God plays any role in morality, it is a secondary or supportive one (Gyekye 2010). Based on the metaphysics of ATR, however, we propose an account where God or some divine property is foundational in morality, namely, the property of vitality.

Second, when we talk of '*African* religious ethics', we understand our project to be a philosophical one in that we aim to extract crucial intellectual resources in African cultures, specifically vitality that is a pervasive onto-moral property in many of them, and to subject it to philosophical analysis in order to produce an ethical theory. As stated in our introduction, our project is not an anthropological one, where we aim merely to represent or report on African people's actual moral beliefs, a project that occupies much of the scholarship on African ethics. Instead, our project aims at a rational interpretation of moral resources associated with ATR that ought to appeal to anyone, if they are convinced by our construction of a vitality-based interpretation of ethics. We use the idea of *religion*, in religious ethics, to refer specifically to a spiritual property that serves as the foundation for morality, one whose source, identity, and function are inherently God-centred. For our part, we posit vitality as the relevant God-centred property.

5.3 Vitality and Its Ontology

To construct an African religious ethic, we will rely on important ontological features or characteristics of its ontology that will help us to grasp the centrality of vitality (see also Section 1). Our reading of the literature suggests a trilogy of ontological features will help to understand vitality and its role in ethics, namely: metaphysical monism; metaphysical holism, and the nature/function of vitality.

5.3.1 Metaphysical Monism

By 'metaphysical monism' we mean that typical African metaphysics under-stands the world to be composed of both natural and supernatural things (Gbadegesin 2005, 415–6). 'Natural' refers to things we could investigate or understand by appealing at the very least to our senses or by recourse to scientific techniques. On the other hand, 'supernatural' refers to things in principle beyond our senses and scientific techniques such as God and ancestors. The African tradition espouses an ontological system that embraces both the natural and supernatural as part of a single whole (Okeja 2013, 112). There is no dualism, but a single realm of reality characterized by a duality of properties: the natural (perceptible) and supernatural (imperceptible). As noted in 2.5, this type of ontological picture is quite distinct from the one found in the Abrahamic faiths, and we believe leads to a unique ethical theory that deserves further attention.

5.3.2 Metaphysical Holism

The African metaphysical system construes reality in holistic terms. 'Metaphysical holism' is the view that interprets reality in terms of how things hang together and function together in a world. Typically, concepts of interdependence or interrela-tions are central in holistic approaches. Bénézet Bujo, an authority on African anthropology and Christian discourse, informs us that 'Africans do not think in "either/or", but rather in "both/and" categories' (2001, 3). Heidi Verhoef an American scholar of moral education observes in a study of African morality, 'Everything – God, ancestors, humans, animals, plants and inanimate objects – is connected, interdependent and interrelated' (Verhoef and Michel 1997, 395). With this ontological system, reality is essentially relational: things live and thrive and even are to be identified only in relationships with others. The holism associated with African thought sheds light on why African cultures tend to prize the community highly, and their cultural and moral systems are characterized as communitarian (Mbiti 1970).

5.3.3 The Function of Vitality

The holism characteristic of African thought has been deployed by scholars to give an account of the cosmic order. For example, scholars of African thought tend to characterize the cosmic order in terms of a *hierarchy* (see also 1.4). As Laurenti Magesa, an influential theologian from Tanzania, states, 'In the conception of African religion, the universe is a composite of divine, spirit, human, animate and inanimate elements, hierarchically perceived, but directly related, and always interacting with one another' (Magesa 1997, 39, see also Imafidon 2014b; Mbiti 1970; Shutte 2001). We can categorize the hierarchy into two groups: the supernatural, which is higher, and the natural which is lower. Even within the supernatural, we have God that occupies the highest position, followed by ancestors below him. Human beings lie at the centre of the hierarchy, and so occupy the highest position in the natural domain. Below them follows animals (and all animate things) and after animals follow the vegetal, and finally inanimate things such as rocks at the bottom of the hierarchy. What informs the structure and positions of things in the hierarchy?

Vitality explains the positions of things in the hierarchy. 'Vitality' refers to that divine energy or (life)-force that emanates from God and maximally inheres in him, which pervades all living and non-living things in the world (Bikopo and van Bogaert 2010, 44). Vitality defines the essence of divinity in one major strand of African thought (see Metz and Molefe 2021). Moreover, all existing things participate in divinity because God has distributed a measure of vitality in them, albeit in varying degrees and complexities. The supernatural realm possesses higher levels of vital energy or life force, the human possesses higher than animals, and so on. The notion of 'life' as used here differs from that common in the Western tradition, which traces genetic factors or some such biological feature or the idea that human beings are created in the image of God (for such Western accounts see Metz 2012a, 24). In African thought, in contrast, life as a spiritual energy is conceived as a sacred gift that characterizes every object.[35] In this light, we note that vitality defines the essence of divinity as the ground of the universe. Vitality explains the hierarchy and the position of each category of existing things in it.

5.4 The Metaethics of Vitality

The major reason scholars of African ethics provide for rejecting the possibility of religious ethics is that African religion is not a revealed religion (Gyekye 2010). It is true that African religion is not 'revealed', at least, not in the way 'revelation' is typically understood within the Abrahamic faiths. For example, revelation in the Christian model of religious ethics plays the critical role of explaining how we access moral knowledge about God's will. The revelation, via the holy scripture, in principle accessible to all human persons, serves the important epistemological function of informing its adherents about the will of God. DCT presupposes exactly this kind of revelation model to define rightness and wrongness relative to the (revealed) God's command (Joyce 2012: 49). In this section we propose an account of metaethics grounded in the ontology of ATR that does not require revelation before showing how it fares better in certain respects than DCT.

5.4.1 Vital Energy as Metaethical Grounds

We suggest that a novel way to construe African religious ethics does not require revelation in order to take root. A vitality-based metaethical system posits vital force as the basis of moral properties or normativity. Note how scholars of African thought posit vitality or life as the basis for morality in African thought. Magesa, states that 'the sole purpose of existence . . . is to seek life . . . to see to it that human life continues and grows to its full potential' (1997, 52). Bujo informs us that 'life is the highest principle of ethics' (2001, 2, 3). He then proceeds to assert that '[t]he main goal of African ethics is life itself . . . The life which issues from God becomes a task for all human beings to accomplish: they must ensure that this initial gift of life reaches full maturity' (Bujo 2001, 88). Placide Temples, famous for being the first person from Europe to apply the title 'philosophy' to African thinking, also states of Bantu people that 'their purpose is to acquire life, strength or vital force . . . Each being has been endowed by God with a certain force, capable of strengthening the vital energy of the strongest being of all creation: man. Supreme happiness, the only kind of blessing, is, to the Bantu, to possess the greatest vital force'

---

[35] In African languages, the concept of *seriti* and *isithunzi* captures the idea of vitality. These words are analogous to the spiritual. Just a like a tree, for example, has *umthunzi* (a shadow), a human being has *isithuzi*, a spiritual or invisible shadow.

(1959, 30, 32). Bujo puts the matter to rest when he states that '[s]trengthening and the growth of life are the fundamental criteria also in the realm of ethics' (Bujo 1998, 27).

There is little doubt that the good in much of ATR is defined in terms of the divine property of vitality. Suppose for a moment that vital energy is indeed the highest good. The good, on this view, is a function of possessing and positively relating to vitality. Possession of vital force is an indication of and indeed is constitutive of, goodness. Rightness and wrongness are functions of how one relates to vitality. Positive relation to vitality is an instance of rightness; and a negative relation to vitality is an instance of wrongness. The aforementioned scholars insist that morality is a function of how we relate to life, where they prescribe that we have to nurture or perfect it. To begin to explain 'positive' and 'negative' relationship to vitality, it is important that we understand that death is the greatest evil in this moral system (Bujo 2005).

Death of the self or person is generally associated with a loss of all vital force. We can understand death in processual and absolute terms (see Bujo 2005, 425). Death as a 'process' refers to a gradual loss of vital force and 'absolute death' refers to a total loss of vital force (not the extinction of the body, since it is thought the self can persist without the body (Bikopo and van Bogaert 2010, 46).[36] The aim of this moral system is the evasion of death by all means both as process and absolute. Thus, a 'positive' relation to vitality refers to a situation wherein the agent preserves and nurtures her vitality, while a 'negative' relation to vitality refers to a situation where one fails to preserve and nurture her vitality, where she would slip into a process of death. In this light, we can define rightness as a function of preserving or growing life and wrongness as a function of a loss of life. The growth or nurturing of life is associated with pro-social virtues (Shutte 2001). The dissipation of life is associated with things like disease and drought, which might ultimately lead to absolute death.

5.4.2 Vital Energy and Divine Command Theory

The rough sketch provided earlier of a vitality-based metaethical system immediately dispels the requirement for revelation in order to have a legitimate religious ethical system. In the ontological framework of ATR, where life is the characteristic feature of all that exists and life is conceived as the highest good, moral knowledge does not require revelation in the sense associated with

---

[36] The idea of death at play here is not merely the biological fact of death. More accurately it is a moral kind of death that is associated with the agent's deeds and character disposition. An agent that is engaged in negative actions depreciates her vitality, which may ultimately lead to biological death.

DCT. Instead, God's will is encapsulated in the reality of vitality that is in and all around us. Our moral obligations revolve around recognizing and responding positively to vitality, and we can learn of our moral obligations through a variety of methods, sometimes from diviners who are in touch with ancestors, but other times by critically reflecting on the natural order of things

The vitality-based metaethics of ATR appears to compare favourably with one important religious alternative in the Anglo-American tradition as located in DCT. In particular, it seems to do a better job of avoiding the Euthyphro dilemma. The first horn of the dilemma concerns the arbitrary nature of morality if the moral status of divine commands rests entirely on them being commanded by God; that is, it is right because God says it is right. In this light, as in the case of God commanding Abraham to sacrifice Isaac, it would mean that murder is right just because God happens to command it. The second horn of the dilemma gestures at the independence of morality from God, where God commands something because he recognizes it to be right. The implication of this horn of the dilemma suggests that if God commands what is already right then it follows that morality is entirely independent of God.

The vitality-based metaethical account does not require revelation for it to count as a robust ethical system. Moreover, the vitality-based metaethical theory does not appear to be affected by the Euthyphro dilemma because morality entirely pivots on our relation to the divine property of vitality, whether positive or negative, which has no necessary relation to requirements about the following commandments. The basic explanation for morality is a positive relation to vitality. This is because whatever counts as moral is fundamentally grounded in vitality. Morality cannot be independent from God since it entirely derives and relies on the divine onto-moral property of vitality, that is, God's essence as opposed to God's contingent commands.[37]

Many important questions remain. A key claim in our suggestion is that ATR avoids the pitfalls of the Euthyphro dilemma in part because it is not a revealed religion of commands made to use and in part, because it appeals to God's nature as superlatively valuable as what grounds moral obligation. Defending this claim further would involve showing how having a written document from God is different from, say, learning God's nature and hence fixed will through interaction with a departed ancestor. This shows that an interesting way to continue the debate between vitality and revelation-based accounts of morality

---

[37] The real debate between those committed to revelation-based accounts of morality and vitality-based accounts will be in question of which, between the two, offers the most promising account of how to access God's will. The vitality account may avoid the Euthyphro dilemma, but it may do so as a high epistemic cost of not being able to give a robust concerning how we can access knowledge regarding the will of God.

involves questions of moral epistemology. Specifically, one question concerns which of the two approaches offers the most promising account of how to access God's will. Even if the vitality account avoids the Euthyphro problem, it may come at the cost of not being able to offer a plausible account of how to access God's will, which the revelation account appears to do well. Finally, African normative ethics and applied ethics dominate the contemporary literature, leaving a dearth of work in metaethics. Which metaethical theories in the Anglo-American tradition, if any, could be leveraged to ground normative theories offered on the contemporary African scene is an open question.

5.5 Vitality and Human Dignity

The concept of human dignity denotes superlative moral worth (Donnelly 2015). It associates the fact of being human with moral specialness or the highest intrinsic moral value. The kind of moral specialness in question is one that demands and deserves moral recognition in the form of respect. We are aware that the concept of human dignity is a controversial one. On the extreme side of the controversy are those scholars who consider the concept to be useless, and as such they recommend that we jettison it altogether if we are committed to meaningful discussion of morality (e.g., Macklin 2003; Pinker 2008; Singer 2009). We do not take such an extreme position and instead draw a distinction between a *concept* of human dignity and a *conception* of human dignity (see Metz 2012a; Molefe 2022). On the one hand, the concept of human dignity denotes the abstract idea of it, which captures it in terms of the highest moral worth. On the other hand, a conception of human dignity refers to the theory of it, which provides a substantive account of what explains our moral worth. In our view, there is very little dispute at the level of concept that captures the intuition that there is something morally significant or special about human persons relative to, say, rose bushes and mice. The controversy resides at a level of conception where scholars provide different metaphysical bases to ground the moral worth of human beings.

The concept of human dignity gained significance partially due to the Universal Declaration of Human Rights (from here on UNDR). The UNDR imagined a new world order oriented towards peace and prosperity, and it stipulated human dignity as the foundational value that undergirds the new world order (Donnelly 2009). Human dignity indicates the superlative intrinsic value or moral specialness of at least human persons, while human rights serve as political-legal instruments to protect and empower human beings to live under dignified conditions (Hughes 2011). What the UNDR does not do is supply us with a globally uncontroversial conception of human dignity. It appeals to reason and conscience as what grounds dignity (Article 1), but that is a contested view.

In what follows, we explain some influential theories of human dignity, before outlining the vitality-based account of human dignity as one plausible alternative.

5.5.1 Influential Anglo-American Accounts of Human Dignity

Certain scholars account for human dignity in terms of certain ontological features of human beings. Consider this comment by Jeremy Waldron, a leading scholar of human dignity in the Western tradition of philosophy:

> There is the Kantian theory based on autonomous moral capacity, there is the Catholic theory based on humans' being created in the image of God, there is a theory developed by me and others about dignity as a status rather than a value [...] and there is the theory of dignity developed by Ronald Dworkin in Justice for Hedgehogs. (2013, 8)

In this quotation, Waldron identifies four distinct conceptions of human dignity that suggest that some feature of our nature accounts for human dignity. The first two of these conceptions explicitly identify the relevant ontological feature of human nature that accounts for our moral specialness or moral worth. Consider the influential Kantian theory of human dignity that accounts for it by appealing to our autonomous or rational nature. On this view, human beings have moral worth because they have the capacity for autonomy. This would count as a secular view of human dignity because it invokes the natural (or, for Kant himself, non-natural) property of rationality to account for human dignity. The second theory of human dignity mentioned by Waldron is a religious one, which accounts for human dignity by appealing to a spiritual property (i.e., being created in the image of God). The mere fact that human beings are created in the divine image explains their moral worth. Even for Waldron's status approach, according to which we have dignity insofar as we have a certain elevated rank, it is natural to ask why we, and not mice, are entitled to that status. We hope the point is clear that a very common strategy to account for status or intrinsic dignity in the Anglo-American literature tends to appeal to certain distinctive features of our nature (FitzPatrick 2013; Sulmasy 2008).

5.5.2 Vitality-Based Dignity

We now proceed to articulate a vitality-based account of human dignity that contrasts with the brief description of Anglo-American counts just offered. Scholars of African thought present vitality as the basis for human dignity. For example, Pantaleon Iroegbu remarks that vitality 'brings to focus the positive value of life. Because it is divine in resemblance, it must be taken loftly and with the highest respect. It must be seen for what it is: of high value'

(2005, 448). Consider also the comment, 'In the case of Bantu philosophy, the ontological base is the concept of energy, strength, and vital force. It is what gives beings their intrinsic value' (Bikopo and van Bogaert 2010, 44). The positive value of life derives or depends on God. Iroegbu represents life as of high value requiring the highest form of respect towards it. Bikopo and van Bogaert associate the possession of vitality with intrinsic value. At this stage, we can conclude that human beings are intrinsically valuable because they possess vitality, but we have not yet arrived at human dignity. Remember, all that exists in the cosmos possess vitality, which implies that everything, to some degree, possesses intrinsic moral worth.

Everything on the African metaphysical system has intrinsic moral worth since everything possesses some degree of vitality. It is possible to account for human dignity by appealing to the fact that human beings have the highest degree or most complex kind of vitality in the natural domain of the hierarchy. We use the technical notion of moral status to indicate that the thing is intrinsically valuable. In the literature on moral status, it is believed to come in degrees where some things have it partially and others have it fully (e.g., Toscano 2011; Jaworska and Tannenbaum 2019). The degree of an entity's moral status is proportional to the strength of the obligations we have towards it (e.g., Degrazia 2008). The higher the degree of moral status, the more stringent and demanding are the duties we have towards such an entity. Full moral status is tantamount to having a dignity, which is the highest possession of value.

Although everything has moral status in the hierarchy since everything possesses vitality, it is only human beings that have human dignity because they possess the greatest vitality in the natural sphere. 'Life-force varies quantitatively (in terms of growth and strength) and qualitatively (in terms of intelligence and will)' (Anyanwu 1984, 90), where human beings have more power and more complex selves than other perceptible beings. The position that human beings occupy in the hierarchy and the corresponding quantity and quality of vitality secure them high or full moral status. Remember, we have explained that human beings have the most vitality because they occupy the highest position in the natural part of the hierarchy, below only God, lesser divinities, and ancestors who are in the invisible realm. In our account of human dignity, we delimit the scope of our focus on the natural part because of the view that 'the theatre of morality and ethical responsibility is the visible world' (Magesa 1997, 72). By 'visible world', in this instance, we should understand Magesa to be drawing a distinction between the natural and the supernatural spheres of reality. The former is visible and the latter invisible. Though morality has its source in God who is in the supernatural sphere of existence, morality happens in the natural sphere (i.e., in the visible realm) in relation to possession and participation in vitality. That can include ancestors having obligations to promote vital force in the lives of their human descendants (e.g., Wiredu 1992, 144). Human beings are considered to be a morally privileged part of the natural world because they can not only execute the role to nurture and protect vitality with the aim to facilitate harmony in the cosmos but also have their vitality enhanced by others. We hereby conclude discussion of how a vitality-based account explains human dignity by appealing to the fact that human beings possess the greatest vitality in relation to their position in the hierarchy.

5.5.3 Vitality-Based Dignity and Imago Dei

To help assess the plausibility of the vitality-based conception of human dignity, we now contrast it with one important Christian conception of human dignity that accounts for it in terms of *imago dei*. On this Christian conception of human dignity, human beings are morally special because they participate in divinity by being created in the likeness of God. Being created in the likeness of God secures the sacredness of human life.

Before proceeding we first note a crucial distinction between these two theories of human dignity. To appreciate the distinction, Metz (2012a) distinguishes three frameworks within which we could interpret theories of human dignity, namely, individualism, relationalism, and holism. Individualistic accounts of human dignity account for it strictly by appealing to internal characteristics of the individual like a soul, pleasure, basic capabilities, and so on. Relational accounts explain human dignity by appealing to the essential human ability to relate or connect with others. Like individualism, the relational capacity might be an internal characteristic of the individual, but the essential difference would be in the other-orienting nature of the capacity in question that is absent in an individualistic approach. It need not be the relationship that has moral status, although it could be; it might instead be the capacity for it. Holism accounts for human dignity in terms of group membership. By merely being a member of the group, the entity has the same human dignity as any other member of that group without regard to any other ontological capacities she may lack.

In the light of this distinction, we observe that it is reasonable to suggest that *imago dei* is individualistic whereas the vitality-based account of human dignity possesses a holistic element. On the *imago dei* interpretation of human dignity, a person has it because she is actually created, as an individual, in the image of God. To present as human is immediately to be sacred because one is created in the image of God. Though vitality is ultimately a property possessed by an individual, which captures its individualistic component, a fuller understanding of it must not overlook its holistic component. According to vitalism, human beings have dignity because they belong to the stratum that has the highest vitality in the hierarchy. It is merely belonging to this relevant human stratum that ultimately accounts for human dignity. On both views, *all* human beings have equal moral dignity and deserve the utmost moral regard. Where they may differ is that while both have an individualistic aspect, the vitality-based view also emphasizes the holistic aspect.[38]

5.6 Dignity and Bioethics

In this section, we compare and contrast how vitality and *imago dei* addresses various bioethical issues. We limit our focus to beginning and end-of-life issues, specifically on abortion and euthanasia.

5.6.1 Dignity and Abortion

We begin by observing that both accounts appear to forbid abortion. For example, a book dedicated to clarifying the concept of human dignity in the Western tradition observes:

> From the above prohibitions against suicide and abortion, and the equation of artificial means of health care with the right to basic health care, one can assume that God-given dignity makes human life sacred. If dignity forbids suicide, abortion and the removal of feeding tubes, then dignity demands respect for the sanctity of human life. (Schroeder and Bani-Sadr 2017, 47)

The sacredness associated with human being forbids suicide and abortion. *Imago dei* has an essential absolute dimension to it, where it generally forbids all abortion and all instances of suicide. We use the idea of suicide expansively to include both passive and active euthanasia. The underlying moral logic behind *imago dei* is that questions of who is to live and die are outside of the human ethical scope. Although it is impossible for us to kill a soul, an immortal spiritual substance, if we were to abort a human foetus or commit suicide, it would be degrading to those made in the image of God and also disrespectful of God himself. Those questions, at best, are the sole prerogative of God. Abortion and euthanasia are generally forbidden, all things being equal.

On the vitality view, all else being equal, abortion is forbidden. The underlying moral logic for this view revolves around valuing life for its own sake and perhaps the fact that it is possible for a vital force, unlike a soul, to disintegrate. It is crucial to notice, however, that as much as the vitality account has deontological

---

[38] We are aware that Aquinas' talk of different dignities in his hierarchy might also have the implication of holism. Holism is not an aspect that is usually emphasized in modern renditions of *imago dei*; one supposes that might be the case due to the influence of methodological individualism that is also very influential in modern ethical theory, particularly in the West.

constraints, which forbids certain ways of harming or interfering with beings who possess dignity; it also has a *perfectionist* dimension that is usually not emphasized in the *imago dei* view. Recall that earlier we quoted Tempels, indicating that vitality can and should be strengthened, and he also associates the greatest blessing with growing vitality. Scholars of African thought tend to construe the growing of vitality in terms of the pursuit of full humanity, which express itself via other-regarding virtues. For example, Shutte explains the perfectionist element of vitality ethics by claiming that 'our deepest moral obligation is to become more fully human. And this means entering more and more deeply into community . . . the goal is fuller humanity' (2001, 31). The more we relate positively with others in the community, the more we strengthen our vitality which expresses itself through pro-social virtues of sympathy, care, kindness, and so on.

The constraining deontological dimension of vitality, all things being equal, would forbid all killings be it abortion or suicide since such acts violate the divine energy characteristic of our nature and humanity. The fundamental reason why abortion is wrong can be explained both in the deontological and perfectionist dimensions. The deontological dimension forbids it because it fails to recognize the intrinsic and high worth associated with a human being's strong and complex vitality. The perfectionist dimension defines the purpose and function of vitality. In the context where we are sure that the child to be born will not be able to participate in vitality through the pursuit of growth, abortion in this context might be permitted. The insight here is that vitality does place the most emphasis on life itself, which is also regulated by the perfectionist dimension – the ultimate moral purpose of the existence of a human being as a carrier of vitality requires that we grow vitality. In the case of an anencephalic infant, for example, abortion may be permitted because as much as the infant does possess some vitality, she can never participate in the ethical task of nurturing or growing her vital energy. But apart from these extremely rare occurrences, the deontological and perfectionist dimensions forbid abortion. In typical cases, vitality forbids violating a being with dignity, and we have a duty to ensure her arrival on earth so she may participate in the perfectionist purpose of existence.

5.6.2 Dignity and Euthanasia

Whereas *imago dei* also forbids euthanasia, vitality could permit it. The major difference between the two approaches is the role of the perfectionist dimension, which provides a justification for euthanasia. Should a person reach levels of medical deterioration where they can no longer participate in the perfectionist dimension of existence, which is the growing of vitality, then euthanasia is arguably permissible. If we keep in mind that the moral purpose of our existence, as carriers of vitality just is to overcome moral death, which we can achieve by acting in ways that intensifies our vitality, this conclusion becomes clearer. In the case, however, where the medical patient reaches a point where they can no longer participate in the battle against moral death, she has now entered a situation where euthanasia is permissible.

On the *imago dei*, inviolability is unconditional, whereas on vitality one may elect to be killed on the premise that she can no longer enjoy the greatest blessing of intensifying her vitality. The moral intuition underlying the permissibility of voluntary euthanasia is the African mentality of fearing shame. Certain medical conditions, in their extreme manifestation, can be attended by a loss of important human functions that may manifest forms of existence that are characteristically shameful in ways that are antithetical to the perfectionist dimension of vitality. It is this intuition that lies behind leading scholar of African bioethics Godfrey Tangwa's comment that 'At such ripe old age, the Nso' fear illness and suffering but not death' (1996, 195). It is not illness or suffering per se that is feared because in certain instances these could be the means by which to perfect one's character by developing fortitude and courage. It is instead those instances of illness that are not connected with the perfection orientation, which we may classify as pointless illness or suffering or perhaps an unjustified condition of existence that is sometimes characterized by shame. Two possible illnesses where these criteria may (sometimes) be met are perhaps certain types of very advanced late-stage cancer and late-stage amyotrophic lateral sclerosis (ALS).

In sum, according to a vitality-based account, human beings have dignity because they possess the greatest vitality in the natural or visible world. We noted that the vitality-based view of human dignity has both the individualistic and holistic element, and we further noted that it has both deontological constraints and perfectionist (i.e., the goal of growing or perfecting vitality) elements. The difference between it and *the imago dei* view lies largely in that the latter is absolutist and the latter is not when dealing with cases of abortion and euthanasia, where instead it generally forbids the former and permits the latter. These are just two examples of potential interaction between an African religious ethic, and one located in the Anglo-American tradition. Not only do these topics warrant much further consideration but there are numerous other topics in bioethics that deserve careful cross-cultural philosophical analysis.

5.7 Conclusion

This section provided an interpretation of African religious ethics. To construct this picture, it focused on two ethical themes. On the one hand, it articulated a vitality-based account of moral properties, where it accounted for rightness in terms of positive relation to vitality and wrongness in terms of negative relation to vitality. It suggested that we should take seriously a vitality-based metaethics because it grounds a religious ethic on God's nature as opposed to contingently revealed commands, thereby avoiding the Euthyphro dilemma. Our point was not so much that vital energy as a moral theory is necessarily more plausible than DCT, but rather that these putative moral-theoretical advantages warrant it being taken seriously as a metaethical theory on a more global stage.

We then considered a vitality-based account of human dignity that says that humans have dignity because they possess the most amount of or highest sort of vital energy in the natural or visible world. With respect to the bioethical issues of abortion or euthanasia, we noted that it generally forbids abortion (unless under conditions where we are sure beforehand that the foetus, for medical reasons, would not be able to participate in vitality). We also noted that it permits euthanasia in extreme medical conditions where the agent can no longer participate in vitality intensification, but they are left in the realm of unjustified shame.

6 The Afterlife

6.1 Introduction

In this final section, we compare and contrast the version of the afterlife found in the Abrahamic faiths with the one in African Traditional Religion. We focus on highlighting the differences in the length of the afterlife (6.1), the location of the afterlife (6.2), and what precisely occurs in the afterlife (6.3). We show that ATR stands in stark contrast to the more Western traditions as it does not affirm immortality or claim there is a heaven in a spiritual realm (6.4). Though compared to the previous sections we focus less on specific philosophical arguments and more on describing significant differences between these traditions, we conclude by exploring the relevance of such differences for the debate about the meaning of life in the Anglo-American philosophical tradition (6.5). In particular, we suggest that the characteristically African conceptions of the afterlife merit attention as prima facie desirable, given an interest in a meaningful life.

6.2 The Length of the Afterlife

There is a long-standing tradition in all of Islam, Christianity, and (rabbinic) Judaism of a person having an indestructible soul and the self being identical with, or at least contained within, that soul.[39] It, therefore, follows on these traditions, or significant strains of them, that people are 'immortal', by which is

---

[39] Metz and Molefe note that this is so for the Jewish tradition at least in the rabbinic period after Christianity (2021, 404).

meant that they live forever. Though in descriptions of ATR, one does sometimes come across terms such as 'immortal', they do not appear to depict the same concept as it is used in the Anglo-American faiths (Metz and Molefe 2021, 404). In fact, descriptions of 'immortality' often have nothing at all to do with living forever, and instead indicate that a person is part of the living-dead, which means that their disembodied selves continue to live on Earth for a time after bodily death, so long as they are remembered and otherwise treated as part of the family. However, there is typically no expectation that the living dead will be remembered forever, thus 'the word 'immortality' usually suggests an afterlife, but one that is expected to peter out after some time, with talk of four or five generations being salient' (Metz and Molefe 2021, 404; see also Sobukwe 2009, 721). Of the Yoruba people in Nigeria, Molefi Kete Asante confirms this when he writes, 'For the ancestors to be ritually remembered, they have to appear in the memory of the people. Once they are no longer in the memory, they cease to exist for the community' (2009, 231).

Vital energy goes some of the way towards explaining why immortality is not to be expected, because one's vitality is at least partly dependent on one's community ties. Thus, the longer a living dead is remembered, the longer they will live as they are sustained by members of the community through grave visits and listening to divine messages (Metz and Molefe 2021, 404). This means, 'Without the sustaining energy of human beings, the thought is that a member of the living-dead perishes' (Metz and Molefe 2021, 404; see also Jahn 1961, 109; Mbiti 1990, 25; Menkiti 1984, 174).

Metz and Molefe speculate that there are two different reasons why adherents of ATR tend to say the living-dead eventually dies, which means the self no longer exists. First, vital energy is a kind of force and it is natural to think that this energy disintegrates over a long period of time, moving towards chaos (Metz and Molefe 2021, 404). Second, if one's self is fundamentally a relational concept, as is salient in the African tradition, then it is also natural to think that this identity will change over time. An indestructible soul that is not dependent on a relational property like vital energy for its existence is clearly less likely to be influenced by external causes in the world. In sum, 'the African metaphysics of the self is fluid and does not easily make sense of the prospect of eternal life' (Metz and Molefe 2021, 405). However, it is held that the strength of ancestors' vital force is so great as to enable them to live much longer than typical living-dead, perhaps because ancestors are deemed to be closest to God.

6.3 The Location of the Afterlife

The Abrahamic faiths tend to affirm the existence of a transcendent heaven that is otherworldly, existing in an entirely different dimension of reality. Though some versions of Christianity pick up on the ancient Jewish theme of resurrection and believe that God will resurrect the dead and establish a perfect new heaven and earth, this new world will still be entirely distinct and separate from the current one.

The location of the afterlife in ATR is not otherworldly in this sense since, as we have noted elsewhere (1.5), the distinction tends to be between the visible and invisible with both existing in the same universe. This means that '[t]he hereafter is in this view next to this world, and for the majority of people it is situated on the same earth' (1975, 115). When a person dies, they remain part of their community and '[t]heir surviving relatives and friends feel that the departed are close to them' (Mbiti 1975, 117). This helps to explain, in part, why the bodily dead are referred to as the *living* dead. Those whose bodies have recently died are routinely thought to reside at a particular place such as a grave, with gravesite visits being not merely to occasion remembrance of a dead person, but also to visit a person who lives on, albeit in a different, imperceptible form.

6.4 What Happens in the Afterlife

Though the textual information one finds about the afterlife in the Bible, for example, is scant, fairly robust pictures of the afterlife still emerge in the Judeo-Christian tradition. For example, one common idea in Christianity, at least amongst philosophers, is that the afterlife consists of being in the beatific vision forever. This is a state of perfect and direct communing with God. During their earthly life, a person's sin would have separated them from God, making it impossible for them to be directly in the presence of such a holy being. However, upon redeeming the work of Jesus, a person enters the beatific vision in heaven, and is thus in the direct presence of God forever in a state of worship, joy, and, maybe, bliss. We don't pretend this is the only account of the afterlife in the Christian tradition, but these ideas do appear with some frequency throughout Christian thought.

There are striking dissimilarities between the idea of an eternal beatific vision and descriptions of the afterlife on ATR. On ATR when a person dies and becomes a member of the community of the living-dead, they also remain very much a part of their community and are merely invisible. The living-dead who are lucky enough to become ancestors because of their prior, human contributions to the clan are thought to act as mediators between God and humans, and thus continue to serve an important function in the daily lives of those who are still alive. For example, of them, Deji Ayegboyin and Charles Jegede say, 'They are believed to be the closest link between the living and the

Dead, Heaven and Earth. There is a strong belief that the ancestors are benevolent spirits' (2009, 712; see also Mbuvi 2009, 23). However, the living-dead generally are not thought to be constantly in the direct presence of God, even if ancestors are thought to be able to receive messages from God.

In sum, in the Abrahamic faiths, it is typically thought that once a person's body dies they leave the world and enter an entirely distinct spiritual realm and ideally becomes present before God, while on ATR a person becomes a member of the living-dead, staying where they are and remaining very much a part of their community. Libations are poured out for them and they are told of family happenings, while those in the imperceptible realm are meant to continue to help human family members as they can.

6.5 The Afterlife and the Meaning of Life

In this section, we explore how differences between the Abrahamic and ATR conceptions of the afterlife impact the meaning of life. The time for such cross-cultural engagement about meaning is ripe as Anglo-American philosophers have taken up the meaning of life over the last twenty years or so, while the topic has only just recently been examined in its own right in professional African philosophy. With respect to the Anglo-American literature, two basic camps have emerged in supernatural and naturalist positions about meaning. Extreme supernaturalists claim that God is necessary for a meaningful life (see Craig 1994; Cottingham 2005; Waghorn 2014). For example, God assigns a purpose to humans that they ought to fulfil and without which their lives would be meaningless. Moderate supernaturalists claim that though God is not necessary for meaning, he would *enhance* it if we related to God in a certain way (see Cottingham 2016; Goetz 2012). On the other hand, moderate naturalists say that a meaningful life is possible even if God (or a soul) would enhance one's meaning. Extreme naturalists say that God or a spiritual realm would render our lives meaningless.[40]

In contemporary African religion and philosophy, most of the literature explicitly discussing the meaning of life has been published within the last few years. As with the Anglo-American tradition, there are so far two major positions about meaning, also following the supernaturalist (imperceptible agency) versus naturalist (perceptible) distinction. Within both of these camps, there is the view that life is meaningful inasmuch as it promotes community (i.e., harmony) with others. Supernaturalists conceive of the community as including the living-dead and ancestors and perhaps as a destiny

---

[40] There is also a debate about whether the standards for meaning are subjective or objective, but we will not enter into that here and instead simply assume objectivism.

prescribed by God, while naturalists are of course secular, suggesting that it is entering into community with other humans and perhaps animals that counts. Second, and more pertinent for our purposes, is the view that a life is meaningful inasmuch as it promotes vitality in oneself and others (advanced by Agada 2020b; held by Metz 2020 to be the strongest of characteristically African approaches), with supernaturalists conceiving of vitality in terms of a divine energy, but naturalists focusing on the physical properties of biology and psychology. This theory of meaning is the one that most obviously emerges from ATR. Metz explains that:

> Sometimes the focus is on developing vitality in oneself, traditionally to the point where one's vital-force is so strong as to become an ancestor. Other times the thought is that one should foster vitality in others in order to live meaningfully, such that one's purpose is to produce in them properties such as health, growth, reproduction, creativity, vibrancy, activity, self-motion, cour-age, and confidence. Correspondingly, one's purpose is also to reduce in others properties that include disease, decay, barrenness, destruction, leth-argy, passivity, submission, insecurity, and depression. I suppose here that the most promising account of meaning in life includes both oneself and others and relevant sites of liveliness. (2020, 119)[41]

Such a theory is able to make 'some good sense of the meaningfulness of friendships, clubs, and the like, insofar as participation in them is expected to make people more active and feel stronger. Relationships appear meaningful particularly when there is a mutual enlivening between people, where loneliness is normally stultifying as opposed to stimulating' (Metz 2020, 120).

Though a lot of the religious-philosophical discussion on the meaning of life focuses on the impact of God, there are closely related questions about what impact an afterlife, especially an eternal one, would have on meaning. Consider that monotheism is perfectly consistent with there being no afterlife at all, as per a plain reading of much of the Hebrew Bible (particularly Genesis and Ecclesiastes), or at least different conceptions of an afterlife.[42] It seems that implicit in much of the discussion of meaning and God amongst contemporary Western religious philosophers is the idea of an afterlife. Supposing that the conception of God in question is relevantly similar between the Abrahamic faiths and ATR at least with respect to meaning,[43] one important question becomes how their significantly different versions of the afterlife bear on meaning.

---

[41] For more on vitality and self-regarding duties see Metz (2022, 81).

[42] On the reasonable assumption that monotheism does not logically entail that humans have indestructible souls.

[43] This may well be a fairly large assumption, but we wish to focus questions about the afterlife.

One relevant difference in this case regarding meaning and the afterlife is the one of length. ATR's conception of the afterlife typically lasts a handful of generations while the Judeo-Christian tradition usually posits an eternal afterlife. The question of whether immortality would have a positive, negative, or neutral effect on meaning has received some attention in the Anglo-American literature. Bernard Williams famously argues that an immortal life would detract from meaning because it would eventually become boring (1993). However, Lisa Bortolotti and Yujin Nagasawa counter that this is not the case because it is possible to experience and enjoy certain goods numerous times (i.e., there are 'repeatable' goods, in the influential terms of John Martin Fischer) (2009). Metz suggests that engaging in boring tasks so that others do not have to take them on can plausibly contribute to meaning (2012b). Another salient concern about immortality is repetition, with an eternal life that repeats itself looking unattractive to many from the standpoint of meaning. Our point here is neither to summarize nor to adjudicate the literature Williams' claim has generated, but instead to observe that it is far from uncontroversial that immortality is better than mortality.

The distinction between immortality and mortality that is often in view may well be one between the usual length of an earthy life (eighty years or so if we are lucky) and a life that does not end. However, what has not been discussed very often in the Anglo-American literature on meaning is the idea of significant *life extension*,[44] which is just what the ATR offers us. Consider that one such implication of a finite afterlife is that it could provide God with the ability to dole out justice in the afterlife or enable people to finish major projects while simultaneously avoiding any of the potential disvalue of immortality. In exploring related ideas, Metz and Molefe conclude, 'Perhaps the African view of the afterlife, or something close to it, can obtain the advantages without the disadvantages: there would be enough time for retributive or compensatory justice to be meted out, and yet not so much time as to drain a life of novelty and growth' (Metz and Molefe 2021, 406). Of course, which conception of justice one has in mind could matter here as African ethics tends to eschew retribution in favour of reconciliation. Either way, these ideas suggest the basis for further cross-cultural dialogue between ATR and the Abrahamic faiths about the role that the afterlife plays in meaning.

In addition, while many in the Judeo-Christian tradition would welcome meeting their maker, those in the African would question whether that is even possible, given God's nature and ours. If it were possible, they would also

---

[44] For a discussion of the value of life extension in the context of meaning see Weinberg (2015) and Lougheed (2023).

question whether it would be desirable quite so soon after bodily death. Might it not be preferable to stay in touch with family, at least for a while?

6.6 Conclusion

The conception of the afterlife one generally finds in the Abrahamic faiths contrasts sharply with descriptions of the afterlife in ATR. On the former, many hold that there is an indestructible soul such that the self necessarily lives forever, while on the latter it is natural to think that if one is made up of vital energy, eventually it will break down. Instead of going to heaven (or hell) in a different spiritual realm, ATR suggests that when a person dies, they become a member of the living-dead, and remain very much a part of their community, with those who become ancestors serving as a conduit between God and living humans. Anglo-American philosophers of religion have debated whether immortality would have a positive, negative, or neutral effect on the meaning of life. However, the type of afterlife posited by ATR, which is a kind of life-extension, has not been sufficiently explored in connection to meaning and other areas of value theory. That ATR is a monotheistic religion that appears to deny immortality is a strikingly unique position in itself, at least compared to much of what one finds in the Western tradition and should be considered by scholars more broadly across the globe.

7 Only the Beginning for Global Philosophy of Religion

The purpose of this Element has been to introduce the readers to the main features of ATR (Section 2), before exploring points of similarities and contrast to the contemporary Anglo-American philosophy of religion. In Section 3: Arguments for the Existence of God, we examined two versions of the cosmological and teleological arguments. Regarding the former, we tentatively concluded that even though ATR may be consistent with the PSR, it is not consistent with the doctrine of creation *ex nihilo*. With respect to the latter, we noted that the ATR doctrine of creation *ex materia* shows why it is easy for the proponent of ATR to endorse classical design arguments for God's existence. Whether it is also consistent with the more recent fine-tuning arguments remains to be seen because such consistency hinges on whether multiverse theories are compatible with ATR. Section 4: Arguments against the Existence of God surveyed three prominent arguments for atheism in the problem of divine hiddenness, the problem of no best world, and the problem of evil. We concluded that the problem of divine hiddenness may well be more solvable on ATR because God is thought to be more distant and separated from humans than is typical in the Abrahamic faiths. Since ATR appears to affirm that God creates the best possible world, it does not have a readymade answer to the problem of no best world. We also examined a number of possible solutions to the problem of evil, tentatively concluding that ATR seems consistent with many responses common in the Anglo-American tradition. In Section 5: African Religious Ethics, we explored the possibility of developing a metaethical theory based on vital energy. We suggested that it fared better than the Divine Command Theory in the important respect of avoiding the Euthyphro dilemma. We concluded by examining a conception of dignity based on vitality, comparing it to the one grounded on *imago dei* and suggesting their implications for bioethical controversies probably differ. Finally, in Section 6: The Afterlife, we claimed that the life-extension suggested by ATR's conception of the afterlife might allow God to dole out appropriate punishments thereby making the universe (more) just while simultaneously avoiding any of the problems associated with immortality. The implications of ATR's conception of the afterlife have not been sufficiently explored in the Anglo-American religious-philosophical tradition.

We readily admit that the arguments and themes we discussed in these sections were fairly generic versions such as one may find in a textbook. We took this approach not only in order to make this Element accessible to non-specialists, but also in order to keep it to a manageable size. For instance, discussing each of the classical arguments for God's existence or non-existence, or important conceptions of dignity, in relation to ATR could easily each take up a full-length monograph on their own. This is not to mention that we did not even discuss many relevant arguments both for and against God's existence or examine every metaethical framework or theory of dignity. Our work in this Element, then, is just the beginning for the comparative philosophy of religion between the African and Anglo-American traditions.

We conclude by once again emphasizing to the reader that this Element is introductory, exploratory, and tentative. Our main goal has been to show that there is fruitful cross-cultural dialogue to be engaged in between the African philosophy of religion and the Anglo-American philosophy of religion. We believe we have just scratched the surface of potential topics, and hope readers will take up future comparative projects. We also believe that our success in showing the potential for productive comparative work is a point that gener-alizes to the African and Anglo-American philosophical traditions beyond the philosophy of religion. Finally, the African philosophical tradition is just one of many that have been largely ignored in the Anglo-American philosophical tradition. We therefore hope that this Element will provide an example of one way of conducting cross-cultural philosophy, not just in order to expand the uptake of African philosophy, but also to prompt consideration by those working in the Anglo-American tradition of other oft-neglected philosophical traditions, particularly those of the East and global South. We look forward to philosophy becoming a more truly global discipline.

References

Achebe, C. (1994). *Things Fall Apart*. Palatine, IL: Anchor

Adams, R. M. (1972). 'Must God Create the Best?'. *The Philosophical Review*, 81(3), 317–32.

Agada, A. (2020a). 'Grounding the Consolationist Concept of Mood in the African Vital Force Theory'. *Philosophia Africana*, 19, 101–21.

Agada, A. (2020b). 'The African Vital Force Theory of Meaning in Life'. *South African Journal of Philosophy*, 39, 100–12.

Agada, A. (2022a). 'Rethinking the Concept of God and the Problem of Evil from the Perspective of African Thought'. *Religious Studies*. First View, 1–17.

Agada, A. (2022b). 'Bewaji and Fayemi On God, Omnipotence and Evil'. *Filosofia Theoretica*, 11(1), 41–56.

Almeida, M. (2018). *Cosmological Arguments*. Cambridge: Cambridge University Press.

Almeida, M. J. (2012). 'The Logical Problem of Evil'. *Midwest Studies in Philosophy*, 36(1), 163–76.

Anyanwu, K. C. (1984). 'The Meaning of Ultimate Reality in Igbo Cultural Experience'. *Ultimate Reality and Meaning*, 7, 84–101.

Aquinas, T. (2012). *Summa Theologiae*. Steubenville: The Aquinas Institute.

Aristotle. (2018). *Physics*. C. D. C. Reeve (Eds.). Indianapolis: Hackett.

Asante, M. K. (2009). 'Egungun'. In M. K. Asante & A. Mazama (Eds.), *Encyclopedia of African Religion* (pp. 231–233). Thousand Oaks: Sage.

Attoe, A. D. (2022). *Groundwork for a New Kind of African Metaphysics: The Idea of Predeterministic Historicity*. Cham: Palgrave Macmillan.

Ayegboyin, D., & Jegede, C. (2009). 'West African Religion'. In M. K. Asante, & A. Mazama (Eds.), *Encyclopedia of African Religion* (pp. 711–13). Thousand Oaks: Sage.

Balogun, O. A. (2009). 'The Nature of Evil and Human Wickedness in Traditional African Thought: Further Reflections on the Philosophical Problem of Evil'. *Lumina*, 20, 1–20.

Behrens, K. G. (2014). 'Toward an African Relational Environmentalism'. In E. Imafidon & J. A. I. Bewaji (Eds.), *Ontologized Ethics: New Essays in African Meta-Ethics* (pp. 55–72). Lanham: Lexington Books.

Bewaji, J. A. I. (1988). 'Human Knowledge and the Existence of God'. In C. S. Momoh. (Eds.), *Nigerian Studies in Religious Tolerance*, Vol. IV (pp. 243–70). Lagos: CBAAS/NARETO, John West.

Bewaji, J. A. I. (1998). 'Olodumare: God in Yoruba Belief and the Theistic Problem of Evil'. *African Studies Quarterly*, 2, 1–17.

Bikopo, D. B. & van Bogaert, L.-J. (2010). 'Reflection on Euthanasia: Western and African Ntomba Perspectives on the Death of a Chief'. *Developing World Bioethics*, 10(1), 42–48.

Bortolotti, L., & Nagasawa, Y. (2009). 'Immortality without Boredom'. *Ratio*, 22(3), 261–77.

Boyd, G. A. (2001). *Satan and the Problem of Evil: Constructing a Trinitarian Warfare Theodicy*. Downers Grove: InterVarsity Press.

Bujo, B. (1998). *The Ethical Dimension of Community: The African Model and the Dialogue between North and South*. C. Namulondo (Trans.). Nairobi: Pauline's Publications Africa.

Bujo, B. (2001). *Foundations of an African Ethic: Beyond the Universal Claims of Western Morality*. New York: The Crossroad.

Bujo, B. (2005). 'Differentiations in African Ethics'. In W. Schweiker (Ed.), *The Blackwell Companion to Religious Ethics* (pp. 419–34). Oxford: Blackwell.

Chemhuru, M. (2014). 'The Ethical Import in African Metaphysics: A Critical Discourse in Shona Environmental Ethics'. In E. Imafidon, & J. A. I. Bewaji (Eds.), *Ontologized Ethics: New Essays in African Meta-Ethics* (pp. 73–88). Lanham: Lexington Books.

Chimakonam, A. (2022). 'Why the Problem of Evil Might Not Be a Problem after All in African Philosophy of Religion'. *Filosofia Theoretica*, 11(1), 27–40.

Chimakonam, J. O., & Chimakonam, A. E. (2022). 'Examining the Logical Argument of the Problem of Evil from an African Perspective'. *Religious Studies First View*, 1–14.

Chimakonam, J. O., & Ogbonnaya, L. U. (2021). *African Metaphysics, Epistemology, and a New Logic*. Cham: Palgrave Macmillan.

Clarke, S. (1705) [1998]. *A Demonstration of the Being and Attributes of God and Other Writings*. E. Vailati (Ed.). Cambridge: Cambridge University Press.

Copan, P., & Craig, W. L. (2017). *The Kalam Cosmological Argument, Volume 2: Scientific Evidence for the Beginning of the Universe*. London: Bloomsbury Academic.

Copan, P., & Craig, W. L. (Eds.). (2019). *The Kalam Cosmological Argument, Volume 1: Philosophical Arguments for the Finitude of the Past*. London: Bloomsbury Academic.

Cordeiro-Rodrigues, L. (2022). 'Christianity in the Kingdom of Kongo and Western Theism: A Comparative Study of the Problem of Evil'. *Philosophia Africana*, 22(1), 13–27.

Cordeiro-Rodrigues, L., & Agada, A. (2022). 'African Philosophy of Religion: Concepts of God, Ancestors, and the Problem of Evil'. *Philosophy Compass*, 17(8), e12864.

Cordeiro-Rodrigues, L., & Chimakonam, J. O. (2022). 'The Logical Problem of Evil and African War Ethics'. *Journal of Military Ethics*, 21(3–4), 272–85.

Cottingham, J. (2005). *The Spiritual Dimension: Religion, Philosophy and Human Value*. Cambridge: Cambridge University Press.

Cottingham, J. (2016). 'Meaningfulness, Eternity, and Theism'. In J. Seachris, & S. Goetz (Eds.), *God and Meaning* (pp. 123–36). New York: Bloomsbury Academic.

Craig, W. L. (1979). *The Kalām Cosmological Argument*. London: Palgrave Macmillan.

Craig, W. L. (1994). 'The Absurdity of Life without God'. In J. Seachris (Ed.), *Exploring the Meaning of Life: An Anthology and Guide* (pp. 153–72). Malden: Wiley-Blackwell.

Cullison, A. (2010). 'Two Solutions to the Problem of Divine Hiddenness'. *American Philosophical Quarterly*, 47(2), 119–34.

DeGrazia, D. (2008). 'Moral Status as a Matter of Degree'. *The Southern Journal of Philosophy*, 46, 181–98.

Donnelly, J. (2009). *Human Dignity and Human Rights*. Denver: Josef Korbel School of International Studies.

Donnelly, J. (2015). 'Normative Versus Taxonomic Humanity: Varieties of Human Dignity in the Western Tradition'. *Journal of Human Rights*, 14, 1–22.

Dopamu, A. P. (1986). *Èṣù, the Invisible Foe of Man: A Comparative Study of Satan in Christianity, Islam, and Yoruba Religion*. Ijebu-Ode, Nigeria: Shebiotimo.

Dougherty, T. (2016). 'Skeptical Theism'. In E. N. Zalta (Ed.), *The Stanford Encyclopedia of Philosophy*. https://plato.stanford.edu/archives/win2016/entries/skeptical-theism/.

Dougherty, T., & McBrayer, J. P. (Eds.) (2016). *Skeptical Theism: New Essays*. Oxford: Oxford University Press.

Draper, P., & Schellenberg, J. L. (Eds.) (2018). *Renewing Philosophy of Religion*. Oxford: Oxford University Press.

Dumsday, T. (2012). 'Divine Hiddenness as Divine Mercy'. *Religious Studies*, 48(2), 183–98.

Dumsday, T. (2021). 'Platonism about Abstracta'. *Philosophia Christi*, 23(1), 141–58.

Dunnington, K. (2018). 'The Problem with the Satan Hypothesis: Natural Evil and Fallen Angel Theodicies'. *Sophia*, 57(2), 265–74.

Dzobo, N. (1992). 'Values in a Changing Society: Man, Ancestors, and God'. In K. Wiredu, & K. Gyekye (Eds.), *Person and Community*; Ghanaian

Philosophical Studies, I (pp. 223–40). Washington, DC: Council for Research in Values and Philosophy.

Ehiakhamen, J. O. (2014). 'Beyond Culpability: Approaching Male Impotency through Legitimated Adultery in Esan Metaphysics'. In E. Imafidon, & J. A. I. Bewaji (Eds.), *Ontologized Ethics: New Essays in African Meta-Ethics* (pp. 97–106). Lanham: Lexington Books.

Fayemi, A. K. (2012). 'Philosophical Problem of Evil: Response to E.O. Oduwole'. *Philosophia: International Journal of Philosophy*, 41(1), 1–15.

FitzPatrick, W. J. *"Worth/Dignity" in The International Encyclopedia of Ethics* (Edited by H. LaFollette, pp. 5546–5553). Oxford: Blackwell.

Gale, R. M., & Pruss, A. R. (1999). 'A New Cosmological Argument'. *Religious Studies*, 35(4), 461–76.

Gale, R. M., & Pruss, A. R. (2002). 'A Response to Oppy, and to Davey and Clifton'. *Religious Studies*, 38(1), 89–99.

Gbadegesin, S. (1991). *African Philosophy: Traditional Yoruba Philosophy and Contemporary African Realities*. American University Studies 5.5. New York: Peter Lang.

Gbadegesin, S. (2005). 'Origins of African Ethics'. In W. Schweiker (Ed.), *The Blackwell Companion to Religious Ethics* (pp. 413–23). Oxford: Blackwell.

Goetz, S. (2012). *The Purpose of Life: A Theistic Perspective*. New York: Continuum.

Gould, P. (Ed.). (2014). *Beyond the Control of God? Six Views on The Problem of God and Abstract Objects*. London: Bloomsbury Academic.

Guthrie, S. (2017). 'A New Challenge to a Warfare Theodicy'. *Journal of Philosophy and Theology*, 5(2), 35–43.

Gyekye, K. (1987). *An Essay on African Philosophical Thought*. New York: Cambridge University Press.

Gyekye, K. (1992). 'Person and Community in African Thought'. In K. Wiredu, & K. Gyekye (Eds.), *Person and Community: Ghanaian Philosophical Studies, 1* (pp. 101–22). Washington, DC: Council for Research in Values and Philosophy.

Gyekye, K. (1995). *An Essay on African Philosophical Thought: The Akan Conceptual Scheme*. Philadelphia: Temple University Press.

Gyekye, K. (2010). 'African ethics'. In E. N. Zalta (Ed.), *The Stanford Encyclopedia of Philosophy*. http://plato.stanford.edu/archives/fall2011/entries/african-ethics.

Hamminga, B. (2005). 'Epistemology from the African Point of View'. In B. Hamminga (Ed.), *Knowledge Cultures: Comparative Western and African Epistemology* (pp. 57–84). Amsterdam: Rodopi.

Hasker, W. (1992). 'The Necessity of Gratuitous Evil'. *Faith and Philosophy*, 9, 23–44.

Henry, D. (2001). 'Does Reasonable Nonbelief Exist?' *Faith and Philosophy*, 18(1), 75–92.

Hick, J. (1978). *Evil and the God of Love*. New York: Harper and Row.

Howard-Snyder, D. & Howard-Snyder, F. (1994). 'How an Unsurpassable Being Can Create a Surpassable World'. *Faith and Philosophy*, 11(2), 260–268.

Horsthemke, K. (2015). *Animals and African Ethics*. New York: Palgrave Macmillan.

Hughes, G. (2011). 'The Concept of Dignity in the Universal Declaration of Human Rights'. *Journal of Religious Ethics*, 39, 1–24.

Idowu, E. B. (1973). *African Traditional Religion: A Definition*. London: SCM Press.

Imafidon, E. (2014a). 'On the Ontological Foundation of a Social Ethics in African Traditions'. In E. Imafidon, & J. Bewaji (Eds.), *Ontologized Ethics: New Essays in African Meta-Ethics* (pp. 37–54). Lanham: Lexington Books.

Imafidon, E. (2014b). 'Life's Origin in Bioethics: Implications of Three Ontological Perspectives: Judeo-Christianity, Western Secularism, and the African Worldview'. In E. Imafidon, & J. A. I. Bewaji (Eds.), *Ontologized Ethics: New Essays in African Meta-Ethics* (pp. 133–49). Lanham: Lexington Books.

Iroegbu, P. (1995). *Metaphysics: The Kpim of Philosophy*. Madison: International Universities Press.

Iroegbu, P. (2005). 'Do All Persons Have a Right to Life?' In P. Iroegbu, & A. Echekwube (Eds.), *Kpim of Morality Ethics: General, Special and Professional* (pp. 78–83). Ibadan: Heinemann Educational Books.

Jahn, J. (1961). *Muntu: An Outline of Neo-African Culture*. M. Greene (Trans.). London: Faber and Faber.

Jaworska, A., & Tannenbaum, J. (2019). 'The Grounds of Moral Status'. In E. Zalta (Ed.), *The Stanford Encyclopedia of Philosophy*. The Metaphysics Research Lab, Center for the Study of Language and Information, Stanford University, Stanford. https://plato.stanford.edu/entries/groundsmoral-status/.

Joyce, R. (2012). 'Theistic Ethics and the Euthyphro Dilemma'. *Journal of Religious Ethics*, 30, 49–75.

Kasenene, P. (1994). 'Ethics in African Theology'. In C. Villa-Vicencio, & J. de Gruchy (Eds.), *Doing Ethics in Context: South African Perspectives* (pp. 138–47). Cape Town: David Philip.

Kelly, S. E. (1997). 'The Problem of Evil and the Satan Hypothesis'. *Sophia*, 36(2), 29–32.

Kraay, K. J. (2011). 'Theism and Modal Collapse'. *American Philosophical Quarterly*, 48(4), 361–72.

Kraay, K. J. (2013). *The Problem of Divine Hiddenness*. Oxford Bibliographies Online.

Kraay, K. J. (Eds.). (2015). *God and the Multiverse: Scientific, Philosophical, and Theological Perspectives*. New York: Routledge.

Leibniz, G. (1709) [1952]. *Theodicy*. A. Farrer (Ed.), & E. M. Huggard (Trans.). New Haven: Yale University Press.

Leibniz, G. (1714) [1991]. *The Monadology*. Pittsburgh: University of Pittsburgh Press.

Lougheed, K. (2022). 'The Epistemic Benefits of Diversifying the Philosophy of Religion'. *European Journal for Philosophy of Religion*, 14(1), 77–94.

Lougheed, K. (2023). 'Benatar and Metz on Cosmic Meaning and Anti-natalism'. *The Journal of Value Inquiry*.

Mackie, J. L. (1982). *The Miracle of Theism: Arguments for and against the Existence of God*. London: Oxford University Press.

Macklin, R. (2003). 'Dignity Is a Useless Concept'. *BMJ*, 327, 1419–20.

Magesa, L. (1997). *African Religion: The Moral Traditions of Abundant Life*. New York: Orbis Books.

Martin, M. (1983). 'God, Satan, and Natural Evil'. *Sophia*, 22(3), 43–4.

Mbiti, J. (1970). *Religions and Philosophy*. New York: Doubleday.

Mbiti, J. S. (1975). *Introduction to African Religion*. Long Grove: Waveland Press.

Mbiti, J. S. (1990). *African Religions and Philosophy*. 2nd ed. Oxford: Heinemann.

Mbuvi, A. M. (2009). 'Akamba'. In M. K. Asante, & A. Mazama (Eds.), *Encyclopedia of African Religion* (p. 23). Thousand Oaks: Sage.

Menkiti, I. (1984). 'Person and Community in African Traditional Thought'. In R. Wright (Ed.), *African Philosophy: An Introduction* (3rd ed., pp. 171–181). Lanham: University Press of America.

Metuh, E. I. (1981). *God and Man in African Religion*. London: Geoffrey Chapman.

Metz, T. (2007). 'Toward an African Moral Theory'. *Journal of Political Philosophy*, 15, 321–41.

Metz, T. (2012a). 'African Conceptions of Human Dignity: Vitality and Community as the Ground of Human Rights'. *Human Rights Review*, 13, 19–37.

Metz, T. (2012b). *Meaning in Life: An Analytic Study*. Oxford: Oxford University Press.

Metz, T. (2020). 'African Theories of Meaning in Life: A Critical Assessment'. *South African Journal of Philosophy*, 39(2), 113–26.

Metz, T. (2022). *A Relational Moral Theory: African Ethics in and beyond the Continent*. Oxford: Oxford University Press.

Metz, T., & Molefe, M. (2021). 'Traditional African Religion as a Neglected Form of Monotheism'. *The Monist*, 104, 393–409.

Molefe, M. (2022). *Human Dignity in African Philosophy: A Very Short Introduction*. Cham: Springer.

Morriston, W. (2003). 'Must Metaphysical Time Have a Beginning?'. *Faith and Philosophy*, 20(3), 288–306.

Mulago, V. (1991). 'Traditional African Religion and Christianity'. In J. Olupona (Ed.), *African Traditional Religions in Contemporary Society* (pp. 119–34). New York: Paragon House.

Murove, M. F. (2007). 'The Shona Ethic of Ukama with Reference to the Immorality of Values.' *Mankind Quarterly*, 48 (2): 179–189.

Njoku, F. O. C. (2002). *Essays in African Philosophy, Thought and Theology*. Nekede: Claretian Institute of Philosophy.

Ofuasia, E. (2022). 'An Argument for the Non-Existence of the Devil in African Traditional Religions'. *Filosofia Theoretica*, 11(1), 57–76.

Okeja, U. (2013). 'Postcolonial Discourses and the Equivocation of Expertise'. *Philosophia Africana* 15(2), 107–116.

Oppy, G. (2000). 'On A New Cosmological Argument'. *Religious Studies*, 36(3), 345–53.

Oppy, G. (2002). 'Arguing about the Kalam Cosmological Argument'. *Philo*, 5(1), 34–61.

Oppy, G. (2006). *Arguing about Gods*. Cambridge: Cambridge University Press.

p'Bitek, O. (1971). *African Religions in Western Scholarship*. Nairobi: Kenya Literature Bureau.

Paley, W. (1867). *Natural Theology: Or Evidences of the Existence and Attributes of the Deity Collected from the Appearances of Nature*. Boston: Gould and Lincoln.

Paris, P. J. (1995). *The Spirituality of African Peoples: The Search for a Common Moral Discourse*. Minneapolis: Augsburg Fortress.

Penner, M. A. (2006). 'Divine Creation and Perfect Goodness in a "No Best World" Scenario'. *International Journal for Philosophy of Religion*, 59, 25–47.

Pinker, S. (2008). 'The Stupidity of Dignity'. *The New Republic*, 28 May. https://newrepublic.com/article/64674/thestupidity-dignity.

Plantinga, A. (1989). *God, Freedom, and Evil*. Grand Rapids: Eerdmans.

Plato. (1997). *Complete Works*. J. M. Cooper (Ed.). Indianapolis: Hackett.

Pruss, A. R. (2006). *The Principle of Sufficient Reason: A Reassessment*. Cambridge: Cambridge University Press.

Pruss, A. R., & Gale, R. M. (2005). 'Cosmological and Design Arguments'. In W. J. Wainwright (Ed.), *The Oxford Handbook of Philosophy of Religion* (pp. 116–137). Oxford: Oxford University Press.

Rachels, J., & Rachels, A. (2010). *The Elements of Moral Philosophy*. Boston: McGraw Hill.

Ramose, Mogobe B. (1999). *African Philosophy through Ubuntu*. Harare: Mond Books.

Rea, M. (2016). 'Gender as a Divine Attribute'. *Religious Studies*, 52(1), 97–115.

Rees, M. (1999). *Just Six Numbers*. New York: Basic Book.

Rowe, W. L. (1968). 'The Cosmological Argument and Principle of Sufficient Reason'. *Man and World*, 2, 278–92.

Rowe, W. L. (1979). 'The Problem of Evil and Some Varieties of Atheism'. *American Philosophical Quarterly*, 16(4), 335–41.

Rowe, W. L. (2004). *Can God be Free?* Oxford: Oxford University Press.

Schellenberg, J. L. (1993). *Divine Hiddenness and Human Reason*. Ithaca: Cornell University Press.

Schellenberg, J. L. (2013). 'A New Logical Problem of Evil'. In J. P. McBrayer, & D. Howard-Snyder (Eds.), *The Blackwell Companion of the Problem of Evil* (pp. 34–48). Oxford: John Wiley & Sons.

Schellenberg, J. L. (2015). *The Hiddenness Argument: Philosophy's New Challenge to Belief in God*. Oxford: Oxford University Press.

Schroeder, D., & Bani-Sadr, A. (2017). *Dignity in the 21st century Middle East and West*. New York: SpringerOpen.

Shutte, A. (2001). 'Ubuntu: An Ethic for a New South Africa'. Pietermaritzburg: Cluster.

Sindima, H. (1989). 'Community of Life'. *The Ecumenical Review*, 41, 537–51.

Singer, P. (2009). 'Speciesism and Moral Status'. *Metaphilosophy*, 40(3–4), 567–81.

Sobukwe, D. (2009). 'Winti'. In M. K. Asante, & A. Mazama (Eds.), *Encyclopedia of African Religion* (pp. 718–24). Thousand Oaks: Sage.

Sogolo, G. S. (1993). *Foundations of African Philosophy: A Definitive Analysis of Conceptual Issues in African Thought*. Ibadan: Ibadan University Press.

Stump, E. (1993). 'Aquinas on the Sufferings of Job'. In E. Stump (Ed.), *Reasoned Faith* (pp. 328–57). Ithaca: Cornell University Press.

Sulmasy, D. (2008). 'Dignity and Bioethics: History, Theory, and Selected Applications'. In The President's Council on Bioethics, Human dignity and bioethics: Essays commissioned by the President's Council (pp. 469–501). Washington, DC.

Swinburne, R. (1979). *The Existence of God*. Oxford: Clarendon Press.

Tangwa, G. (1996). 'Bioethics: An African Perspective'. *Bioethics*, 10, 183–200.

Tempels, P. (1959). *Bantu Philosophy*. C. King (Trans.). Paris: Présence Africaine.

Toscano, M. (2011). 'Human Dignity as High Moral Status'. *Ethics Forum*, 6, 4–25.

Tutu, D. (1999). *No Future without Forgiveness*. New York: Random House.

Ubah, C. N. (1982). 'The Supreme Being, Divinities and Ancestors in Igbo Traditional Religion: Evidence from Otanchara and Otanzu'. *Africa* 52(2), 90–105.

Unah, J. I. (2014). 'Finding Common Grounds for a Dialogue between African and Chinese Ethics'. In E. Imafidon, & J. A. I. Bewaji (Eds.), *Ontologized Ethics: New Essays in African Meta-Ethics* (pp. 107–20). Lanham: Lexington Books.

Uzukwu, E. E. (1982). 'Igbo World and Ultimate Reality and Meaning'. *Ultimate Reality and Meaning*, 5, 188–209.

van Inwagen, P. (2006). *The Problem of Evil*. Oxford: Oxford University Press.

van Inwagen, P. (2009). *Metaphysics*. Boulder: Westview Press

Verhoef, H. & Michel, C. (1997). 'Studying Morality within the African Context'. *Journal of Moral Education*, 26, 389–407.

Waghorn, N. (2014). *Nothingness and the Meaning of Life: Philosophical Approaches to Ultimate Meaning through Nothing and Reflexivity*. London: Bloomsbury.

Waldron, J. (2013). 'Is Dignity the Foundation of Human Rights?' *NYU School of Law, Public Law Research Paper No. 12-73*.

Weinberg, R. (2015). 'Why Life Is Absurd'. *New York Times*, 11 January. https://archive.nytimes.com/opinionator.blogs.nytimes.com/2015/01/11/why-life-is-absurd/?mcubz=1.

Williams, B. (1973). 'The Makropulos Case: Reflections on the Tedium of Immortality'. In B. Williams (Ed.), *Problems of the Self* (pp. 82–100). Cambridge: Cambridge University Press.

Wiredu, K. (1998). 'Toward Decolonizing African Philosophy and Religion'. *African Studies Quarterly*, 1(4), 17–46.

Wiredu, K. (1992). 'Death and the Afterlife in African Culture'. In K. Wiredu & K. Gyekye (Eds.), *Person and Community: Ghanaian Philosphical Studies* (pp. 137–152). Washington, DC: The Council for Research in Values and Philosophy.

Wykstra, Stephen (1984). The Humean obstacle to evidential arguments from suffering: On avoiding the evils of "appearance". *International Journal for Philosophy of Religion* 16(2), 73–93.

Acknowledgements

Kirk Lougheed would like to thank Motsamai Molefe and Thaddeus Metz for their willingness to work with him on this project. He would also like to thank his colleagues at LCC International University for creating a supportive environment for him to pursue research endeavours. In particular, thanks to Romuladas Babarskas, Michael Cox, Joe Harder, Benjamin Groenewold, Chris Howard, Mark Sargent, Tricia Van Dyk, Steve Van Zanen, and Marlene Wall. Thanks also to his research assistant, Lika Beradze, for help with citations and proofreading. He is also grateful for research support from the Department of Philosophy at the University of Pretoria. Finally, thanks to two anonymous peer reviewers for providing helpful comments on the Element. Lougheed's work on this project was made possible, in part, by a research grant from the Council for Christian Colleges & Universities.

Thaddeus Metz is grateful to his colleagues Kirk Lougheed and Motsamai Molefe for joining him in the project of approaching African philosophy of religion not merely comparatively, but also analytically. Thanks also go to the editors of the Cambridge Element series as well as to two thoughtful anonymous reviewers for Cambridge University Press. In addition, acknowledgement is due to the University of Pretoria and specifically the Department of Philosophy for facilitating the composition of this work.

Motsamai Molefe would love to express immense appreciation to Kirk Lougheed for playing a leading role in this project. I would also love to thank Thaddeus Metz for his wisdom and guidance in the project. It is always an honour to collaborate with colleagues who are committed to contributing to global thought drawing from fountains of wisdom from Africa. I am also grateful for the recent contributions towards African philosophy of religion by contemporary African philosophers such Ada Agada, Jonathan Chimakonam, Aribiah Attoe, and Luis Rodrigues.

Cambridge Elements ≡

Religion and Monotheism

Paul K. Moser
Loyola University Chicago

Paul K. Moser is Professor of Philosophy at Loyola University Chicago. He is the author of *God in Moral Experience*; *Paul's Gospel of Divine Self-Sacrifice*; *The Divine Goodness of Jesus*; *Divine Guidance*; *Understanding Religious Experience*; *The God Relationship*; *The Elusive God* (winner of national book award from the Jesuit Honor Society); *The Evidence for God*; *The Severity of God*; *Knowledge and Evidence* (all Cambridge University Press); and *Philosophy after Objectivity* (Oxford University Press); coauthor of *Theory of Knowledge* (Oxford University Press); editor of *Jesus and Philosophy* (Cambridge University Press) and *The Oxford Handbook of Epistemology* (Oxford University Press); and coeditor of *The Wisdom of the Christian Faith* (Cambridge University Press). He is the coeditor with Chad Meister of the book series *Cambridge Studies in Religion, Philosophy, and Society*.

Chad Meister
Affiliate Scholar, Ansari Institute for Global Engagement with Religion, University of Notre Dame

Chad Meister is Affiliate Scholar at the Ansari Institute for Global Engagement with Religion at the University of Notre Dame. His authored and coauthored books include *Evil: A Guide for the Perplexed* (Bloomsbury Academic, 2nd edition); *Introducing Philosophy of Religion* (Routledge); *Introducing Christian Thought* (Routledge, 2nd edition); and *Contemporary Philosophical Theology* (Routledge). He has edited or coedited the following: *The Oxford Handbook of Religious Diversity* (Oxford University Press); *Debating Christian Theism* (Oxford University Press); with Paul Moser, *The Cambridge Companion to the Problem of Evil* (Cambridge University Press); and with Charles Taliaferro, *The History of Evil* (Routledge, in six volumes). He is the coeditor with Paul Moser of the book series *Cambridge Studies in Religion, Philosophy, and Society*.

About the Series

This Cambridge Element series publishes original concise volumes on monotheism and its significance. Monotheism has occupied inquirers since the time of the Biblical patriarch, and it continues to attract interdisciplinary academic work today. Engaging, current, and concise, the Elements benefit teachers, researchers, and advanced students in religious studies, Biblical studies, theology, philosophy of religion, and related fields.

Cambridge Elements ≡

Religion and Monotheism

Elements in the Series

Necessary Existence and Monotheism: An Avicennian Account of the Islamic Conception of Divine Unity
Mohammad Saleh Zarepour

Islam and Monotheism
Celene Ibrahim

Freud's Monotheism
William Parsons

Monotheism in Christian Liturgy
Joris Geldhof

Monotheism and the Suffering of Animals in Nature
Christopher Southgate

Monotheism and Social Justice
Robert Karl Gnuse

Monotheism and Narrative Development of the Divine Character in the Hebrew Bible
Mark McEntire

God and Being
Nathan Lyons

Monotheism and Divine Aggression
Collin Cornell

Open Theism
Alan R. Rhoda

Jewish Monotheism and Slavery
Catherine Hezser

African Philosophy of Religion and Western Monotheism
Kirk Lougheed, Motsamai Molefe, and Thaddeus Metz

Printed in the United States
by Baker & Taylor Publisher Services

.